Kari Mirabal

YOU ALREADY HAVE THE NO

FROM THE KEYNOTE
Naked Networking

FIRST EDITION

Prepared for publication by www.40DayPublishing.com

Cover design by Jonna Feavel

www.40DayGraphics.com

Printed in the United States of America

Start where you are.

Contents

Foreword

By Marcus Aurelius Anderson
TEDx and International Keynote Speaker, Host of "Conscious
Millionaire Epic Achiever Show", Peak Performance Mindset
Coach and Author of "The Gift of Adversity"

Why do people dread networking?

Because it sucks.

I take that back—it sucks because of the way the majority of people approach networking. Some actually think handing out business cards hoping they'll be remembered, while simultaneously debating which cards they'll actually keep or inevitably throw in the trash, is what networking is. This type of networking is a huge waste of time. But like so many things in business today, outdated and antiquated mindsets "because that's how it's ALWAYS been done" remains comfortable for far too many people. If you're sick of that type of interaction, *YOU ALREADY HAVE THE NO, Naked Networking* is the right read for you.

Kari Mirabal and I are fortunate to have many things in common. We're both TEDx speakers, respected leaders, innovators, and coaches in each of our respective fields of expertise. Kari dominates the networking and career development space while I attack business with brutally honest soul-searching methods to discover the gift of adversity. If you've ever witnessed her keynotes, participated in her masterclasses, or partnered with her through coaching programs, you already know that Kari doesn't know a stranger. Her genuine spirit of authenticity and infectious enthusiasm for networking inspires so many. Kari initially introduced herself to me using the segue of our mutual respect for Roman emperor and philosopher Marcus Aurelius, my namesake. She introduced herself to a perfect stranger and as a result, we've witnessed how the YOU ALREADY HAVE THE NO approach really works, for those brave enough to embrace fear and take calculated risks.

Kari helps you alleviate the trepidation of networking while sharing easily replicated steps that teach you how to network smarter. Most people have heard the dated business phrase, "your network is your net worth" but that's not true. I believe a global collection of successful people's contact information is worthless if an authentic relationship wasn't built along the way. With the fake, bloated numbers of "followers" on social media today, we've all seen this proven, over and over again. When you receive and contribute incredible value engaging with others, the true answer to creating mutual benefit and reciprocity for everyone involved is the ultimate reward. That's the kind of network that improves your net worth, and that's exactly what Kari teaches in this book.

Most speakers who talk about networking barely scratch the surface, but Kari built her business developing relationships, giving back, and truly caring about people's success. She speaks from experience and influences others to work outside comfort zones and to consider new possibilities. Authentic networking encourages you to do more than just find a new career or succeed in your business; it widens your perspective about the gift of giving. Overall, networking helps you become a better person when you unselfishly contribute to the success of others.

It's why I didn't think twice about writing the foreword for *YOU ALREADY HAVE THE NO, Naked Networking.* I believe in Kari's mission to create a movement of people all dedicated to networking smarter. So read, laugh, grow, and take action to embrace vulnerability; the core muse behind the art of Naked Networking.

Acknowledgements

This book would never have seen the light of day without the help and support of so many amazing people. I am truly thankful for the positive and negative experiences writing this book required me to push through. I started writing *YOU ALREADY HAVE THE NO* during a difficult season of growth in my life—working through epic heartbreak, growing my business in new directions, grieving the loss of my Grandmother Bettye (one of my biggest fans), a car accident, and finding out my dog, Rex, has cancer.

Despite the challenges, I know I'm right where I need to be—learning from each failed experience. I thank God for guiding me through tough days and reminding me I am a woman of value, someone precious in his eyes. Success is earned with each glorious step forward.

Those I'm truly thankful for:

The loves of my life—Justus and Markus Mirabal. Thank you for inspiring me to continue moving forward despite life's challenges. I love you guys with all my heart and soul. I am so very proud of you both. Each of you have unique and amazing gifts—use them for good. Follow your passions and don't give up. Never forget YOU ALREADY HAVE THE NO, go for the ask. Live your dreams. Have faith. I believe the universe has big and beautiful plans for both of you. Be kind to each other. Thanks for all the "un-limit-ids" (not a typo) shared. It is my hope you both will laugh often, love with all your heart, and know your value. Don't settle. Do your best always. Believe in 111 and PHMG.

Thanks to Marcus Aurelius Anderson, show host of "Conscious Millionaire Epic Achiever Show", TEDx speaker, Author of "The Gift of Adversity" and Performance Mindset Coach. He coached me through my best and met me at my worst. He kicked my butt when I needed it and gave me a hug when I felt I couldn't go on. With every voicemail, text, and uplifting word of encouragement, Marcus Aurelius Anderson (www.marcusaureliusanderson.com) helped me stay the course. He reminded me to seek out adversity and use it as a compass to drive myself forward into unchartered territories of new growth and higher achievement.

Thanks to my amazing friends, my sisterhood: Betsy Cox, JoAnn Lair, Shannon Gann, Mandi Lee, Lori Reynolds and the beautiful, Ms. Sherry James for believing in me and never letting me forget who I am. You each encouraged me in your own way to take risks and follow my purpose. For all the laughs you provided, support you extended, tears you shared, and encouragement you never stopped giving, I love you all.

To Stacie Casler, Licensed Professional Counselor, LPC, CCSAS, CCPS and aka "Mom-Lady" of Grace Ventures, LLC, who I owe so very much. I'm thankful the universe intervened, and I never received "the" email you sent. It is your body of work that inspires me to donate a portion of the proceeds of this book to your organization so other women can experience the gift of knowledge and inspiration via scholarship opportunities. (www.gvcounsel.com)

To Dawn McNulty, thank you for dragging me to those networking events I hated, and now love. Thank you for encouraging me to believe in the power of networking.

To all the contacts in my professional network, those who prayed for my success, and for all the participants in my keynote audiences for sharing tips, success and failure stories, and being vulnerable enough to invite me into your space—even for a moment—as you spoke your truth. All of you played a part in my growth because you helped me sharpen my tools as you sharpened yours.

To my wonderful blog readers, LinkedIn, Twitter, Instagram, YouTube, Facebook, and TEDx followers, as well as others in audiences across the country and abroad who convinced me I had something of value to offer the world with every clap, standing ovation, and comments shared on speaker evaluations.

To Nikki Nemerouf, Executive and Leadership Coach with Starquest, Inc. You inspired me to lean into my passion of teaching people how to network smarter. Thank you for your wisdom, encouragement, and all those butt kicks. (www.starquestleadership.com)

To Scott Snyder (Obi-Wan), the proud owner and CEO of Bad Ass Coffee of Hawaii. I am forever grateful for the chances you took believing in me. If it wasn't for that crazy blog years ago, I'm not sure this book would have ever been written. You encouraged me to challenge and believe in myself. I've learned so much about business and life from you. I continue to admire your drive, marketing genius, and overall leadership skills. (www.badasscoffee.com)

To Melissa Munroe Christenson, President of Creative Training Resources (www.creativetrainingresources.com), the stranger I risked talking with on the cruise. Our conversation led to years of business mentoring and friendship. You encouraged me to explore new paths and supported each move forward as my business transformed. You continue to lead by demonstration the importance of holding the bar high. You ROCK.

To all the association leaders and event planners across the US and abroad who believed in me as a keynote speaker for various conferences and corporate events, I thank you for supporting my message and helping me establish a platform to serve as a conduit for others to learn.

To the manager I worked with at my first job, Bob from Ryan's Steakhouse. To this day, I continue to leverage what you taught me about customer service, integrity, and the power of kindness.

To Jay Stillwell of Verizon. Your leadership taught me to believe in myself. You inspired me to lead others, challenge myself, and have fun working outside comfort zones. I feel blessed you continue to be a trusted contact in my professional network.

To other transformational coaches who motivate me; the powerful team at 5-Sisters Ranch, Dana Reynolds, Kyle Cease, Marisa Peer, Richard Branson, Scott Stratten, and Dr. Rhonda Freeman. Your knowledge continues to push me through difficulties as I pursue my speaking business. I've learned so much from your expertise and I am motivated by your success.

64%—Thank you for everything. Atoka.

To the brethren of CR, SLAA, and the trauma group sisterhood of Grace Ventures, LLC, as well as members of Owasso & OKC Sisters Life Groups of www.Life.Church who fight the fight each day—you are some of the bravest people I've ever met. Your persistence, support, and advice lift me up.

Todd Hunter, owner of the "Little House" for providing a safe haven and sanctuary from the storm for my family and me to fail, grow, and learn inside of.

To Christian Derr of Clinch Martial Arts Academy (www.teamclinch.com) for coaching, mentoring, and transforming my oldest son from a boy to a man.

The "Mullet Team," for always making me smile.

To my family in Orlando, FL. Thank you for your support from across the miles. I love you. To my two smart, witty, talented, and amazing beautiful nieces—never quit and know you ARE ALWAYS ENOUGH.

To the Mirabal's and all my awesome nieces and nephews. Thank you for your continued personal and professional support as well as prayers.

Chapter 1
Introduction

"Do one thing every day that scares you."
- Eleanor Roosevelt

"It'll be fun," Dawn said. "I seriously doubt it!" I barked back. My heart pounded as beads of sweat formed on my brow in anticipation of attending yet another networking event. *I hate this shit,* I thought to myself as I stuffed business cards in my purse and walked out the door. I had already decided I would only stay 15 minutes. Besides, I'm way too busy to waste time networking. I ran through my usual excuses to reinforce a negative attitude during the drive to the event—playing victim felt so comfortable. Dawn, a trusted and respected account manager with an eagle-eye for identifying opportunities, felt the opposite of me. Dawn had a knack for lighting up a room, and although I had mad respect for her skills, I also thought she was a bit crazy. *How could talking to strangers possibly be engaging, fun, or helpful?* The thought of talking to people I didn't know terrified me. My mind wandered to the usual anxieties. *What would I say? How much small talk is too much? Could I manage rejection? Is there something in my teeth?* Sometimes I would fantasize about talking to new people. What did I have to lose? However, it never took me long to talk myself out of taking action. The fear was just too intense. Networking made me feel raw, overwhelmed, exposed, vulnerable … naked. Turns out, feeling naked ended up being one of the best things that ever happened to my career and to my life.

Now, I know that networks are powerful things. They can help you get from point A to point B—faster. Plain and simple, networking is about developing mutually beneficial relationships. While there are many benefits to networking, I get how some people feel intimidated and avoid the process altogether. I've been there. I'm not there now. That's why I decided to write this book.

@KariMirabal
Networking is about developing
mutually beneficial relationships.

While the word naked in the book title piques curiosity, it's an acronym for five common barriers that prevent networking breakthroughs. If your current networking process isn't working, I can help you. First, you will have to commit to taking new risks, considering new possibilities, and pushing past fear to connect with confidence.

In this book, I'll show you ways to leverage both traditional and social media networking strategies. We'll explore how to make powerful first impressions and ways to build and maintain impressive networks. While everyone wants the benefit networks often provide, most aren't willing to invest in the work required to achieve the desired result. If you're up for the challenge, this book will help. Soon enough, you'll get comfortable being uncomfortable.

How I Earned My Stripes

In my experience as a former IT recruiter, career coach, TEDx presenter, business owner, and keynote speaker, I've helped countless professionals learn how to network smarter. My youngest client is eighteen and my most "seasoned" client is seventy-two. They both have the same problem; neither knows what they want to be when they grow up. While they share the same challenge, they also share the same solution. Both will have to build and sustain an active network as they seek new possibilities.

I coach college students all the way up to seasoned C-suite executives and love every minute of it. Isn't it exciting to consider how each contact you meet has the potential to change your career and/or life? What adventures lie ahead? I present corporate workshops, keynotes, and coaching services to eager professionals across the country and abroad. Some of my clients include Microsoft, Ball Aerospace, McKesson, Turner Broadcast Systems, MassMutual, American Airlines, Oklahoma University, Oklahoma State University, TTCU Federal Union, the Project Management Institute, and various career workforce, sales, HR, and recruiting conferences, to name a few.

@KariMirabal
Isn't it exciting to consider how each contact you meet has the potential to change your career and/or life?

Networking benefits everyone regardless of title, industry, or company size. I've gathered data, explored why fear paralyzes us at times, and researched why talking to strangers can be daunting. I've learned so much about networking that I just had to write *YOU ALREADY HAVE THE NO*, a look at how taking calculated risks can pay off. I'm on a mission to create a movement of people who network smarter. In this book, I will share both positive networking experiences and epic fails. You're not alone if you've ever felt uncomfortable with the thought of approaching and communicating with strangers. I've made mistakes, but the lessons learned were worth it. I am thankful for my failures. They helped me hone my skills, retool my strategies, and reset direction when I wasn't achieving my desired results.

Today, I grace stages across the country and abroad at conferences and events with some of the best speakers and professionals in their craft. I am passionate about networking because it changed my life and I know it can change yours too.

@KariMirabal
I am on a mission to create a movement
of people who network smarter.

Most people would agree that networking has it perks. Discovering career opportunities, even those in the "unpublished job market," and meeting like-minded people to exchange ideas are just a few benefits. Let's not forget that networking can also play a role in boosting interests or goals in your personal life (like the time I taught my eight-year-old son how to reach out to Magic Johnson about playing for the LA Dodgers). You'll have to read more to get that scoop.

Adopting the "YOU ALREADY HAVE THE NO" approach in this book invites you to dream, work outside your comfort zone and embrace ideas that, at first, may seem shocking. Buyer beware, I don't coach victims. This book will empower those who have the will but might lack skill at this juncture. If you are full of excuses or unwilling to try new things, best to regift this book to someone else. The material covered here is only for those interested in making big career and life changes.

20

What's Your Excuse?

Over the past 20 years, I've heard every excuse about why people don't network. I've coached men and women (ladies, it's time we step up our game; research shows females have fewer network connections than males in the workplace). I've partnered with extreme introverts and extroverts, and have worked with both young and older people. This stuff works, but don't just take my word for it. Here's what a few clients have to say.

> *"I was extremely pleased with the valuable information I learned from Kari's Naked Networking program. I learned more about fostering relationships and utilizing LinkedIn as a tool to generate new contacts. I went into my work week feeling empowered and equipped with the tools necessary to increase my network and grow my business."*
>
> - Zac Hardin, Project Manager, Arrowhead Consulting
>
> *"In a world where "Networking Is Key to Success" Kari's Naked Networking strategies highlighted the advantages of a powerful network while learning and exploring strategies from seasoned networking. A business professional would be hard-pressed to find a more organized and mature networking resource. I would highly recommend this workshop to anyone looking to hone their networking skills."*
>
> - Jason Hurley, PR Manager, Mid-Continent Insurance Group

While I can't guarantee everyone who reads this book will meet and network directly with the likes of Richard Branson or Arianna Huffington (although I challenge you to aim high), I can promise these solutions will challenge you to view networking differently and tempt you to try new things. With patience and a whole lot of practice, your return on investment will be worth it.

@KariMirabal
I will challenge you to view
networking differently.

Don't delay, or others who are already "networking smarter" will beat you to the punch. Avoid missing out on interviewing for the career you've always wanted or an opportunity to connect with more of your target audience!

So, let's get started on getting you information that can change your life as you begin developing mutually beneficial relationships, RIGHT NOW!

The networking tips and secrets you're about to read have proven results. Each chapter provides new insights that will support your networking journey from uncomfortable to comfortable. You'll get a leg up on the competition, and meet some amazing people along the way. You don't have to feel naked anymore. Are you ready to build a powerful network?

If you follow the strategies revealed in this book, it's highly possible you will enjoy the rest of your life unburdened by networking barriers.

What do you have to lose?

YOU
ALREADY
HAVE
THE
NO

May your life never be the same after you read this book.

Chapter 2
YOU ALREADY HAVE
THE NO

"Leap and the net will appear."
- John Burroughs

Have you ever stumbled upon an unexpected opportunity? Perhaps you heard about a new position through the "unpublished job market" or you were introduced to a valuable mentor. Congratulations! You've witnessed firsthand the power of connection. Networks are compelling things that can help you get from point A to point B—faster. For those brave enough, investing time and energy into the art of networking will be one of the most rewarding experiences you'll ever have.

YOU ALREADY HAVE THE NO—Naked Networking's Muse

Talking to strangers can be intimidating for some, but it can also open the door to life changing experiences. If the thought of talking to strangers makes you feel awkward and uncomfortable or exposed, you're reading the right book. The YOU ALREADY HAVE THE NO mindset shares knowledge from my signature keynote and masterclass, Naked Networking. Its core premise invites you to consider new possibilities while transforming negative perceptions about the word *NO*.

What I mean by YOU ALREADY HAVE THE NO is you're already *not* doing business or networking with the target contact you just identified so what do you have to lose by going for the big ask? It challenges you to think differently, which in turn invites new outcomes. YOU ALREADY HAVE THE NO inspires you to find your brave and take risks like the time Warren Ross, President of the Ross Group, sat next to me on an airplane. This random meeting led to me training his staff on networking and LinkedIn strategies. Ross leads a successful development, engineering, and construction company. If I had listened to the initial lies and negative talk in my head telling me not to bother him or that his company was way too big to want to work with me, I would've missed an awesome partnership with a great company. When you decide to approach a stranger, you're setting the stage for yourself (and others) to create new potential.

Naked Networking 101

If reading a few pages of this book already evokes twinges of networking fear, embrace it. Feeling scared means you're about to do something really brave. Chances are you've experienced what "being naked" (i.e., vulnerable) feels like. More importantly, how are you overcoming those awkward and uncomfortable feelings? Has the networking process inspired you, or does it stop you in your tracks? Sadly, many of us allow barriers to block opportunities that might have led to something truly life changing.

The N.A.K.E.D. acronym represents five common networking barriers; Neglect, Afraid, Knowledge, Engage, and Dedicate. This book shares my story and the stories of amazing clients, partners, friends, and diverse people I've had the chance to meet and work with over the last 20+ years as a business owner and coach. It includes proven strategies, examples of success, and failures from my life's experiences. These personal stories are meant to offer perspectives and different ways to embrace the power of connection. Networking isn't rocket science, but it can be rocket fuel when used as a conduit to build powerful connections. Not all of my ideas, strategies, and examples are a fit for everyone. Take what you like; leave the rest.

Mutually Beneficial Relationships—The Objective of Networking

I'm in the business of helping people develop mutually beneficial relationships. The word relationship is defined in the dictionary as "a state of being connected," yet most people struggle to authentically engage with others. My work is cut out for me. People who network smarter understand the importance of discernment throughout the process. The core of networking is about connection, but there are times when it's best to disconnect from people who are toxic or not invested in the long term. As you experience the gift of networking, you'll notice it may slow down at times, but efforts should never stop. They don't stop when you think you've landed the perfect career, or when you think you already have enough contacts in your Rolodex (a dated method for housing contact information). Smart networkers know it's about finding and building relationships that have the potential to be mutually beneficial sooner or later (that means patience is required; people don't always show their true intentions initially). As they say, it takes two to tango. It's not as difficult as you might think to consider how your skills, connections, knowledge, and/or experience can help others reach their goals. You have to be an opportunist and take the time to consciously be aware of what's happening around you—see the opportunities missed by most. I've come to realize most people over-complicate the networking process. Keep it simple; be a contributor to others and start forming a foundation of paying it forward.

@KariMirabal
Practice, patience, and perseverance pay off.

My Story—Networking and I Weren't Always Besties

I was first introduced to the concept of connecting with others to develop mutually beneficial relationships in my first professional job with MCI (now Verizon). I was employed by a consulting firm that supported fraud research. A handful of employees were selected to participate in the pilot program after passing the necessary screening. My teammates and I learned how to prevent fraud—which meant reducing financial losses for MCI. As the department grew, I was selected for a high-potential future leadership program designed to develop business management skills. While eager to absorb most topics presented in training, I couldn't embrace the lessons dedicated to networking. The idea of talking to strangers seemed overwhelming to me. This was a period when the internet was brand new, smartphones didn't exist, and social media wasn't even a thing. That meant the actions associated with networking had to be done through traditional channels. The entire process intimidated me. I felt uncomfortable, exposed—bare naked.

I observed peers on the leadership team applying what they learned as they feverishly added names to their Rolodexes and met other people with whom to exchange knowledge.

28

Meanwhile I sat idle, paralyzed by my own insecurities about the process.

I actively avoided networking mixers, and when I had to go, I huddled in the corner with the other wallflowers. It was easier to join other anti-networkers who conspired to make fun of those who were making the most of the chance to meet new people. I was young and inexperienced. The idea of connecting with others only resonated with me if it meant getting my best friend, JoAnn, and me into the best dance clubs in St. Louis. Networking simply didn't make sense to me at that time because I lacked the will and the skill.

@KariMirabal
Networking and I are besties now
but it wasn't always that way.

Gumball Machine Mentality

There was a time when I thought networking should work like a gumball machine. Gumball machines return an immediate treat when you put a quarter in—every time. Unfortunately, networking doesn't work like that.

Since I felt naked and I lacked an understanding of networking benefits, I continued to "should" on myself—a big mistake. You must work in reality, not in an imaginary world where everything is always fair. As I watched those around me earn promotions and hear about new jobs through networking, I felt isolated and left behind. It was during this period of my life that I made an intentional decision to shift my mindset. I sucked it up and sought advice from a respected mentor, Jay Stillwell. Jay was my first manager while on the MCI project and the first to encourage me to stretch myself in new ways professionally.

I talked to him about wanting to make the necessary changes to evolve outside my comfort zone. I listened to Jay's advice and set out to apply his networking recommendations. Although eager to apply this knowledge, I failed miserably at my first attempt. I failed because I had unrealistic expectations (i.e., gumball machine mentality). As I continued to test ways to network that felt comfortable for me, I learned there's only one way to network smarter—practice, practice, and practice some more.

Addictions Aren't All Bad

As my career progressed and I transitioned into the IT recruiting field, I quickly learned that my bread and butter depended on my determination, my success with helping companies make and save money, and my ability to network. The core of IT recruiting meant keeping pipelines full of qualified technical talent. The YOU ALREADY HAVE THE NO mindset served me as I took new risks, became more assertive, and let go of feeling afraid to speak my truth. When I changed my perspective on being vulnerable (naked), it helped me realize the value of doing the undesirable to get the desirable. I became addicted to networking with each win. I wanted more and more. The high of success and helping others fueled my motivation. Although I failed in the process many times, I worked through each challenge to transform what was once unfamiliar (talking to strangers) to the familiar. I became addicted to the results networking delivered.

Go Beyond What You Believe Possible

As time progressed, I became comfortable with the YOU ALREADY HAVE THE NO mindset. I expanded and grew professionally. Networking turned out to be a consistent conduit that transformed me from one career opportunity to the next without needing a resume. I discovered the "unpublished job market" was an amazing thing. I thanked the universe for pushing me through my fears to prepare me to receive awesome gifts.

Investing time staying active in my network proved fruitful, but the time came when I felt a calling to do more than just use the tools to help myself. I had to go beyond what I believed possible. It was time to return the favor and help others meet their challenges and overcome roadblocks. I started delivering keynotes, conducting corporate training classes, and working with individual clients to teach more people how to network smarter.

Networking isn't about just taking. More importantly, it's about giving. Everyone experiences a season of giving and a season of receiving. Finding balance between the two opens so many amazing new opportunities. Shattering dated mindsets to experience breakthroughs requires realistic expectations, lots of practice, and dedication. Thinking small didn't serve me well, and it won't serve you well either.

Eager Beavers Be Warned

Earlier in this chapter, I posed the question, "what do you have to lose by going for the ask?" Truth be told, there is something you risk losing…your reputation. While the YOU ALREADY HAVE THE NO mindset empowers you to explore new possibilities, I caution you not to let eagerness trump professionalism.

I was teaching a LinkedIn masterclass at a university when an overzealous student announced his flawed strategy. He told the class that he planned to reach out to CEOs on LinkedIn directly because he didn't want to waste time with the "little people." I smiled as he rambled, knowing that it is more effective to take things slowly and be intentional with each step when developing a networking campaign. That includes a networking campaign on social media.

While the prospect of having access to executive information using LinkedIn is easier in the digital age and may feel tempting, be mindful of professionalism. The YOU ALREADY HAVE THE NO mindset encourages you to go for the ask, but maintain business etiquette in the process. If you come on too strong or are ill prepared, you risk losing all momentum and putting your reputation in peril. You never get another chance to make a positive first impression.

Go Slow to Go Fast

Adopting the YOU ALREADY HAVE THE NO mindset helps empower you to consider new outcomes, but don't discount the "go slow to go fast" adage. Once you've identified your goal (begin with the end in mind), view each small step forward as an opportunity to increase the probability for your success. Starting a networking marketing campaign well below the likes of a company CEO affords you the benefit of learning as much as you can about that company's business and culture. Working your way up the ladder means you create a space to meet valuable contacts that can help you down the road when you revisit them for a referral or for name-dropping purposes. When you finally meet your ideal target contact, mentioning that you "spoke with _____ from the software development department who inspired you to apply because he mentioned how he felt the leadership team really cared about its employees" is a way to feed two birds with one seed. You demonstrate you've done your homework while also mentioning you know people who work there in hopes that the manager will talk to the people with whom you've worked hard to build a rapport. When people who work inside the company put in a good word for you, it helps elevate you to a different status during the vetting process when applying for a job.

While I applaud passion, the student who planned to ignore the "little people" and go straight to the CEO demonstrated the danger of recklessly abusing the "ask and you shall receive" approach.

@KariMirabal
Build valuable contacts as you climb the ladder
in hopes of meeting your target contact.

Do the Undesirable to Get the Desirable

Wayne Gretzky said, "you miss 100% of the shots you don't take," and I couldn't agree more. Give yourself permission to take the chances necessary to experience impactful outcomes. The YOU ALREADY HAVE THE NO mindset means doing the undesirable to reach the desirable. In other words, when you choose to work outside your comfort zone (the undesirable), your chances of obtaining the results you seek (the desirable) improve. Networking won't be easy, but it will be worth it if you dedicate yourself to the practice, patience, and perseverance required for connection success.

There are people waiting on you to bring your unique gifts and contributions to the world. Take a deep breath and dive in to see where the adventure takes you. My hope for you is that you will feel excited to take new risks after you read *YOU ALREADY HAVE THE NO*. As I travel across the country and abroad working with diverse people from various industries, I get excited about the prospect of transforming strangers into warm connections. Channel your nakedness (vulnerability) to experience the gifts which networking offers. Kudos to you for taking the next step in your journey by reading this book. It's time for you to join the movement of people networking smarter.

@KariMirabal
People are waiting for you to
bring your unique gifts to the world.

What do you have to lose?

YOU
ALREADY
HAVE
THE
NO

Chapter 2 Key Takeaways

- YOU ALREADY HAVE THE NO—adopt the mindset and take the 50/50 risk.
- The N.A.K.E.D. acronym represents five common networking barriers; Neglect, Afraid, Knowledge, Engage, Dedicate.
- Expand your perspective—don't let a NO stop your momentum.
- Set realistic expectations—avoid a gumball machine mentality.
- Don't recklessly abuse the "ask"—maintain professionalism.
- Work your way up the corporate ladder—meet amazing people along the way.
- Maintain integrity—treat network referrals with respect and care.
- Do the undesirable—get the desirable.
- Consider how your gifts can help others—share.

Chapter 3
Neglect

"The time to repair the roof is when the sun is shining."
- John F Kennedy

The N.A.K.E.D. acronym represents five common networking barriers; **N**eglect, **A**fraid, **K**nowledge, **E**ngage and **D**edicate. In this chapter, we'll explore the barrier **Neglect.** You'll learn why some people neglect networking, how to create meaningful connections, top benefits networking can provide and more.

Do you want to achieve more right now in your career, your business, or your life? Do you want to learn how to develop mutually beneficial relationships? Do you want to reap the rewards networking can offer? If you answered yes to any of these questions, you're ready to take your networking to the next level.

Networking can be an incredibly valuable investment of your time and effort. It can help you make essential business connections, advance your career, and gather valuable feedback. The importance of networking cannot be overstated, yet so many people still think networking is unpleasant. For some, it can feel exhausting, unauthentic, and, frankly, the thought of standing alone among a sea of strangers is utterly painful.

Why People Neglect Networking

When people acknowledge you as a connector and a trusted resource, your value within your network increases. The higher your value, the more benefits you receive. But if the pros of developing a circle of trusted confidants outweighs the cons, why do so many still neglect networking? One word— excuses.

Making excuses is a subconscious behavior for some that hurts networking performance and overall motivation. Excuses can distract and paralyze networking progress, but many of us are tempted to make them anyway.

We all have egos, and from time to time, your ego steps in and wreaks havoc behind the scenes. Your ego means well. It wants to protect you from circumstances that might evoke potential anxiety, embarrassment, or shame. However, when your ego believes you are moving toward unchartered and/or scary territory, it generates excuses to make you question forward steps. The more anxious or afraid you feel about networking, the more likely your ego will build barriers that can impede connection opportunities.

What's Your Excuse?

To stop making excuses and start taking more action, start by evaluating your current networking habits. Explore where you might be making mistakes and identify areas of opportunity. I've gathered some of the most popular networking excuses. Do any of them sound familiar? Which ones have you used lately to neglect developing meaningful business relationships?

Place a check mark next to any excuse or false story you've told yourself about networking:

- ○ I don't have time to network.
- ○ I might fail.
- ○ If I start networking, I'll have to do it 24/7.
- ○ I'm not in the sales profession, I don't need to network.
- ○ I'm happy at my current job, I don't need to network.
- ○ I'm in the _____ industry, I don't need connections outside my industry.
- ○ Social media networking doesn't work.
- ○ I don't want to come across as desperate.
- ○ I already have enough people in my network.
- ○ I'm still working on perfecting my process.

Excuses Debunked

Becoming aware of excuses in the present is a powerful step toward debunking them. If you identified with some or all the above excuses, you're not alone. Those who want to network smarter know they must practice identifying excuses and shifting perspective to advance networking to the next level.

I hope these examples of ways to debunk common excuses help you make more meaningful connections, strengthen your emotional intelligence, and expand your network community.

I Don't Have Time to Network.

Don't neglect your networking activity until you're desperate—perhaps you've lost your job, or you're applying to graduate school and need references. While difficult to prioritize networking when you're gainfully employed, it does pay in the long run to be proactive. Saying thank you, sending a quick email, or engaging on social media with others can help you stay connected within your network. Test how skipping idle chatter, not playing games on your phone, and staying off Instagram or other social media sites magically creates new pockets of time to increase network activity each day. In the upcoming chapter, Dedicate, you'll learn more ways to network in 15 minutes or less.

I Might Fail.

You might succeed. The only people who fail at networking are those who don't even try. It's normal to feel nervous about potential rejection, but don't let that stop you from taking action. If someone ghosts you or says they aren't interested in helping you, don't take it personally. The more you network, the easier it gets to accept that not everyone sees the value of networking. Keep moving forward. Commit to people equally interested in developing mutually beneficial relationships. Find strategies that work best for you and accept there's no such thing as a perfect networker. Everyone will make mistakes along the way. The YOU ALREADY HAVE THE NO mindset encourages you to go for the ask and see where the adventure takes you. What do you have to lose?

If I Start Networking, I'll Have to Do it 24/7.

I'm a power networker, yet it might surprise you to learn that I don't network with everyone around me, everywhere I go, all the time. While I enjoy meeting new people and exchanging information, even I don't want to network 24/7. When not wearing black dresses and orange heels, you might find me in yoga pants with my earphones on. It's as if I have a "do not disturb" sign on my back. This small act helps me respect boundaries set for quiet time. Carve specific time into your day for deliberate networking to avoid burn out.

I'm Not in the Sales Profession, I Don't Need to Network.

The idea of networking evokes uncomfortable feelings for many people. One of the most common misconceptions is that networking is only for people in the sales profession. While business development professionals leverage networking to help introduce audiences to their products and services, the benefits of connection can benefit everyone.

I'm Happy at My Current Job, I Don't Need to Network.

I've witnessed many stories of clients who sabotaged networking potential because they were happy at their current job. While their intention was to stay employed, their employer had different plans. In today's competitive business market, job security is a thing of the past. You must adopt the mindset that you're the CEO of your career. That means the only security you can rely on is your ability to acclimate quickly when circumstances change. It's not a matter of *if* circumstances will change but rather *when* they will change. When they do, you'll be glad you invested time building and sustaining your network. One day, you'll either want to or have to make a career change. When that day comes, you'll need support from others who can help you get from point A to point B. Choose to be ready.

I'm in the _____ Industry, I Don't Need Connections Outside My Industry.

Do you attend the same networking events and trade shows yearly? While there, do you visit the same companies and contacts repeatedly? While easier and more comfortable to stick with what's familiar, if you don't challenge yourself to expand your network, you risk creating a closed loop of contacts. To network smarter, build and sustain connections with people from diverse industries. You'll open your eyes to fresh ideas and different points of view to help you grow professionally.

Building and maintaining contacts outside your industry is another form of job security. If your industry experiences an economic downturn, the market quickly becomes saturated with too many of the same skilled types. Contacts you've established within different industries can open new career opportunity doors and help you stay a few steps ahead of your competition. Set weekly goals to reach out and introduce yourself to new contacts on LinkedIn—people who are experts in something you know little about yet find interesting. Avoid LinkedIn's algorithms that offer connection suggestions. Be proactive by searching for people you find interesting and believe you can learn something from.

Over time, I became too comfortable in my telecommunications career. I felt excited when a friend introduced me to IT professionals, where I discovered an interest in technology that changed my life. If I had stayed in my comfort zone, I would have missed golden opportunities and valuable career development.

Social Media Networking Doesn't Work.

Networking isn't new; the idea of people helping people has been around since the beginning of time, but the tools to connect have evolved (Remember the Rolodex?). Online networking platforms are changing the way we do business, yet some still complain that tools like LinkedIn don't work. Technically, they're right. LinkedIn itself is just a piece of software, it's the human behind the keyboard that makes the magic happen. Each day, more and more online networking options appear. The choices aren't decreasing, they're increasing, which means online networking isn't going anywhere. Your competition is out there right now navigating online connections to gain a competitive advantage. Don't risk getting left behind due to dated mindsets.

I Don't Want to Come Across as Desperate.

Asking for help isn't a sign of weakness. Most of the best leaders, athletes, instructors, and top professionals turn to mentors and coaches for assistance. Being prepared, sharing your intention, and communicating specific ways you believe your contact can help you are hardly a sign of desperation. None of us can achieve goals 100% on our own. When you demonstrate steps you've already taken to get where you want to go coupled with clear communication and a plan of action, your network contact is less likely to see you as helpless.

I Already Have Enough People in My Network.

There are different schools of thought on this excuse. Some believe you only need a few people in your network to help you reach goals, while others boast on LinkedIn about 10,000+ connections. Neither of these approaches is my style. Instead, I focus on quality, not quantity.

I always believe I can learn something new from anyone I meet. When people approach me at conferences, online, or through introductions, I maintain an open mind and get curious about how I will grow from this connection. My network grows and shrinks weekly because I am not afraid to add or remove connections. I want to surround myself with positive people who inspire me by example, offer solid advice, and share ways they believe I can improve professionally. Who I choose to connect with and learn from depends on where I am at any specific time in my career or in my life.

I'm Still Working on Perfecting My Process.

Focus on pursuit, not perfection, when networking. Like me, I'm sure you too have experienced relationship letdowns. Sometimes people I thought were "perfect" for me ended up letting me down in the most unimaginable ways. Meanwhile, those I may not have had any expectation of stepped up and delivered. Life is messy, and networking is no exception. I often remind myself that setbacks are setups for something amazing to unfold in time.

Time to Act

You've learned two ways to avoid neglecting your network: recognizing excuses and shifting perspective. To empower yourself, invest time to prepare for events, conferences, and meetups. Preparation leads to confidence, and that means going far beyond just packing more business cards to hand out to strangers.

Your research ahead of time will pay off. The YOU ALREADY HAVE THE NO mindset challenges you to identify specific contacts you're interested in connecting with to optimize each experience. When attending in-person network events, follow these guidelines to improve success when meeting target and random contacts.

Network Events—Target Contact Guidelines

1. Explore upcoming networking events that appeal to you professionally or personally. Places to consider include industry specific events, conferences, classes, associations, user groups, volunteer opportunities, or meetups—for example, to connect with like-minded professionals.
2. Once you've identified venue options, begin researching potential connections of interest. Ideas for contacts include speakers, volunteers, leaders, and/or event planners who manage these gatherings.
3. Create a list of target contacts and/or companies you want to meet and exchange information with prior to each networking event.
4. Use LinkedIn to send connection requests to your target contact list. Use this platform to introduce yourself and share your intention for connecting.
5. Prepare a 30-60 second "tell me about yourself" response when asked to share what you do (more about this tool in Chapter 5, Knowledge).
6. Closer to each event date, follow up with your target contact. Invite them to meet you in person sometime during the conference or event. Take charge to suggest a location and restate your intention for wanting to connect.
7. Be respectful of time during your meet and greet with new contacts. If you asked for 10 minutes, keep your exchange to 10 minutes.
8. Offer your business card, ask for theirs, and thank each contact for agreeing to meet with you.
9. Ask new contacts if they're open to staying in touch.
10. Thank them for their time, smile, and shake hands again before parting ways.

11. Find ways to stay on your new contact's radar after the event. Share links to upcoming networking or industry events, suggest articles or books, or follow up with questions pertaining to topics discussed during your initial meet and greet. Demonstrate in your follow-up that you can be a valuable resource in their network.

Challenge Yourself—Set Networking Goals Before Each Event

1. Practice your "tell me about yourself" statement before attending each event.
2. Set an intention to introduce yourself to at least 5 new people at each event.
3. Search for wallflowers and introduce yourself.
4. Smile at everyone you make eye contact with; say, hello.
5. Sit next to people you don't know during meals or session discussions.
6. Ask for business cards, take notes on the back to remember details about each contact you meet.
7. Avoid attaching to one person for too long at any event. Move around, meet new people, and expand your network by introducing yourself to diverse people.
8. Be prepared at networking events to ask questions of others but also to answer questions others may ask of you. Actively listen to responses and stay present. This shows respect to your new contact by giving them the gift of your undivided attention.
9. Ask new contacts who would be a good prospect for them.
10. Find people in the room that exude confidence and introduce yourself. Take mental notes as you learn from their body language, questions, and/or networking style.

11. Thank contacts for their time before moving on to greet the next connection.
12. Follow up with target contacts within a week or two after each event. Suggestions include "John, you mentioned you hired a new software developer when we met at the Evolve You Conference. How have things been going so far with them?"

Networks are Powerful Assets

There's no denying powerful networks are an asset in your professional development. Whether online or in person, when done well, networks provide a competitive edge throughout every stage of your career. It's never too early—or too late—to learn how to network smarter, so don't give up hope.

Let's explore more benefits the power of connection can bring when you choose not to neglect your network.

Opportunities Await in the "Unpublished" Career Market

If you like getting ignored after throwing a resume into the black hole of online job postings, keep doing what you're doing. However, if you're willing to invest the time, the unpublished career market can open amazing doors.

The unpublished career market is a beautiful thing. It's a place where open positions have not yet been published on saturated job boards. You hear about these opportunities from contacts inside your network because employers often ask existing employees for referrals before publishing jobs. They do this because they know birds of a feather flock together. When they ask existing team members for referrals, it's good business sense because chances are, they work and spend

47

personal time with like-minded people. Proactively networking with contacts inside target companies can pay off. While it's up to you to demonstrate your value once an interview is scheduled, networking can be a conduit that helps you discover these possibilities.

One of my former career coaching clients, Matt Boily, is an example of someone who mastered the art of navigating the unpublished career market. With over 20 years of senior leadership experience in the aerospace industry, he suddenly found himself part of an unexpected company-wide layoff after relocating to the greater Seattle area. Within weeks of the layoff, Matt had already identified contacts within a new target company, connected with some of their leadership team, and located a hiring authority for an open position he knew he was overqualified for, but decided to explore anyway. He leveraged the YOU ALREADY HAVE THE NO mindset to take a risk. Matt knew from experience that demonstrating his value (i.e., ways he would help the company make and save money), he would leave a positive impression that might lead to other opportunities. Sure enough, after exchanging information about the Plant Manager position, the interviewer recognized Matt's potential. The hiring manager began vetting Matt for a different position not yet announced to the public. Matt jumped on the opportunity to learn more, and as it turned out, was better suited for that position. If Matt had not put pride to the side and agreed to interview for a lower-level position to get a foot in the door to explore the possibilities, he may not have ever heard about this new position. At the time this book published, Matt was scheduled for a second in-person interview for this new role. He was well on his way to being considered for a position inside the unpublished career market.

In my experience with career coaching and recruiting, I've witnessed Matt's story time and time again. Forward-thinking leaders recognize potential in those who successfully demonstrate value and an ability to contribute to increased productivity and company profits.

Think your job is secure? Think again. Don't risk neglecting your network because unexpected layoffs and terminations happen more often than you think. When they do, you'll want to be just a few calls away from asking trusted network contacts for assistance. To tap into the unpublished career market, you simply can't afford to neglect your network.

Sharpen Your Saw

If you neglect your network, you put yourself at risk to miss opportunities. Meeting professionals—inside or outside your industry—to learn from help you "sharpen your saw" (i.e., your skills) and expand knowledge. Powerful networks are filled with people who share information and honest critiques with those they trust.

Solve Challenges

The problem with challenges is they tend to escalate until there's nowhere left for them to go. The buck must stop somewhere. For those in positions of authority, reaching out to fellow executives or professionals in similar roles can help sort out big workplace problems. Two heads are better than one and increase efficiency for solving unresolved issues. Seasoned contacts willing to lend a hand, help narrow down options, and offer support as you explore best possible solutions.

Professional Introductions

Regardless of your title or industry, you're more likely to discover new opportunities through introductions your network shares than by any other means. Be respectful of all introductions received, even the ones you don't immediately see the value of. Use discernment; don't ask for too much too soon. Invest time and energy cultivating each network contact. Allow a natural courting process to unfold, much like you would a romantic relationship, where trust develops over time.

Be a Contribution—Pay it Forward

People often ask how to be more interesting when talking to new contacts. This is not the right approach. To build and maintain powerful connections, focus on ways you can be helpful to others. When you do, you'll see the quality of each interaction increase. To help you explore ways you can support new contacts, ask them who or what would be a good prospect for their business. Invite them to share what's new in their company or department, then listen with full attention. Inquire about any challenges or struggles they may have. Pay kindness forward without expectation of return. In my experience, acts of kindness return to you one way or another.

Reach Personal Goals

For my son Markus' birthday, I thought it would be fun to invite a baseball player to attend his party. I pictured Markus' friends playing catch with a star athlete, autograph books being signed, and kids asking questions as they dreamed of one day being a professional ballplayer too. I used the YOU ALREADY HAVE THE NO mindset to go for the ask and called the Tulsa Drillers, the local minor league baseball team in the town where I live. When the contact I spoke to at the administration office said no to my idea, I turned to my LinkedIn network for help. I don't take no for an answer too often. One of my network contacts saw my post and reached out with a suggestion. He suggested going to the ballpark early and talking with the players as they signed autographs to gather leads and recruit those interested in inspiring kids. This is exactly how I met Wilin Rosario, the former all-star catcher for the Tulsa Drillers. Lucky for us, Wilin had a heart for helping young players develop, and agreed to volunteer his time. It was the highlight of Markus' birthday party. After this experience, we stayed in touch, and our family served as a contact and friend to Wilin. We helped arrange transportation for his family when they visited, invited him to have homemade meals in our home, and even donated furniture to him and his teammates who shared a small apartment. For those who don't know, life in the minor leagues is not as glamourous as you might think. Lucky for Wilin Rosario, he was drafted to the Colorado Rockies soon after and was kind enough to provide tickets to my family and me whenever we visited Denver. Networking is a gift that keeps on giving when the relationship is built on a mutually beneficial foundation.

Get Where You Want to Go—Faster

Networking can help you get where you want to go—faster. However, if you neglect your network, you are out of sight and often out of mind. I once coached a project manager who was tasked with a deliverable to streamline the end-user experience where he worked. His job was to identify, then implement, a software solution on time and within budget. Luckily, my client had a well-established network of go-to contacts he'd built up from various project manager and technology conferences over the years. Several of his contacts offered help when he reached out for their insights about specific software vendors. Talking with trusted contacts in similar roles helped my client gather intel about both failures and successful case studies. In short, this networking process helped him justify his vendor selection. He also helped his company save money because he asked a referral to introduce him to the vendor under the expectation that he had a set budget for the project. The process helped my client make an informed decision. He saved his company time and money by leveraging knowledge others from his network openly shared.

Gain the Big Picture

A critical component of success in today's business market is your ability to anticipate significant market changes. While nobody has a crystal ball, gathering anecdotal data from diverse sources in your network helps you gain powerful insights. These insights translate to business decisions you make that "move the needle" and help your organization save or make money. Keeping your finger on the pulse where the latest business trends, hiring practices, or technology information is shared by those in your network offers you a competitive advantage.

Advantageous Partnerships

Fruitful partnerships are often the foundation for success in the business world. One of the best reasons to network is to gain referrals. Referrals help you identify and build positive relationships with contacts and companies whose products or services align with your brand. Networking is a win-win for organizations interested in identifying and joining forces with others to grow and prosper.

Break Out of Your Comfort Zone

Webinars are easy to watch from the privacy of your office. YouTube videos don't require you to make small talk. However, choosing the easy route won't serve you in the long run if building and maintaining professional connections is important to you. Growing professionally means taking new risks, and the only way to do that is to stretch yourself. Attend as many in-person networking events as you can to break out of your comfort zone. As the saying goes, "Life begins at the end of your comfort zone."

Find Balance in Communication

Those who dominate conversations at networking events risk coming across as self-important, disinterested in listening to others, and generally annoying. Those who network smarter know that taking turns in the process of sharing information is essential to building rapport with strangers. To gain the most benefit from your network, build a reputation for being a trusted contact. Do this by practicing being self-aware of social cues. If someone sends you the signal that they're bored with the conversation, switch it up and ask them a question. Identify times during networking activities when it's best to speak and/or best to listen.

You Don't Know What You Don't Know

To network smarter, embrace the "you don't know what you don't know" mentality. Diverse perspectives help you explore all angles of a challenge to make informed decisions. Live networking events provide a unique convergence of learning and fun. They set the stage for meeting amazing connections and opportunities to bring fresh ideas back to your business—an investment in both yourself and your company. Set an intention to enjoy the experience of expanding knowledge and closing the gap between what you know and what you don't know.

Accept Delayed Benefits

Most people admit understanding the time required to develop mutually beneficial relationships, yet secretly hold expectations of immediate gratification. In the art of networking, patience is a necessary virtue. Sometimes contacts work quickly in your favor, while other times it's a waiting game. Don't lose hope. Accept delayed benefits; they're part of the networking journey.

In the keynote Naked Networking, I share different examples of why you don't want to neglect your network and how accepting delayed benefits can pay off. One of my favorite stories begins when I was sixteen. My parents set a rule when I started driving: no one drove my vehicle but me. I ignored that rule when the cutest boy in my school asked if he could drive my car. Imagine the look on my face when my parents pulled up right next to us at the four-way stop. Busted! I lost my driving privileges that summer, a devastating thing for a teenager. Fast forward 20 years, and I'm teaching a networking masterclass for a new client in the restaurant business. My client raved and raved about a recent visit to Chicago where he and his wife experienced a restaurant named Girl & The Goat. I smiled as my client shared details about the amazing chef, inspired design, and enlightened hospitality. We live in a small world. Kevin Boehm, my high school friend—the same guy I lost my car over—is a James Beard award-winning restaurateur and co-founder of Boka Restaurant Group. Girl & The Goat is one of Boka Restaurant Group's premier chef-driven restaurants. Recognizing the potential for a connection, I reached out to Kevin and shared my client's feedback. Thankfully, Kevin and I kept in touch over the years. I explained how my client was interested in expanding his family restaurant and inquired if Kevin would be open to answering a few questions with my client. Kevin graciously agreed, as he has always had a heart for mentoring others. Don't miss opportunities to be a conduit for connection because you neglected your network. You never know how your act of kindness might help change someone else's life for the better.

People who network smarter are realistic and accept that time invested meeting new contacts doesn't always pay off. There will be people in the world who don't see the value of networking. They might get your hopes up and offer false promises to be there but ghost you when it counts most. You can't control whether people network with you or not, but you can control how you react when they don't.

When things don't work out the way you'd hoped, let it go. Be impeccable with your word, even when others aren't. Show respect to people who don't deserve it; not as a reflection of their character, but as a reflection of yours. Keep it professional. Continue to move forward, and when you are blessed with an act of kindness from someone in your network, find a way to pay it forward.

This chapter explored why you might neglect networking and showcased benefits when you don't. We discovered how excuses limit possibilities and ways to view barriers from different perspectives. Don't neglect your network. My hope for you is that you will join the movement of people all networking smarter.

What do you have to lose?

YOU
ALREADY
HAVE
THE
NO

Chapter 3 Key Takeaways

- YOU ALREADY HAVE THE NO—adopt the mindset and take the 50/50 risk.
- Identify false stories you've been telling yourself about networking.
- Networking isn't just for sales professionals.
- Networking helps with transition in the "unpublished" career market.
- Networking can help you meet like-minded people.
- Networking can help you make a contribution to others.
- Networking can help you reach personal goals.
- Networking can help you get from point A to point B—faster.
- Networking requires pursuit, not perfection.
- Be prepared before attending networking events.
- Be thankful when acts of kindness appear. Pay it forward.
- Networking sometimes means accepting delayed benefits.

Chapter 4
Afraid

"And the day came when the risk to remain tight in a bud was more painful than the risk it took to blossom."
-Anais Nin

The N.A.K.E.D. acronym represents five common networking barriers including **N**eglect, **A**fraid, **K**nowledge, **E**ngage and **D**edicate. In this chapter, we'll explore the barrier, **AFRAID**. You'll learn why networking scares some people and how to push past fear to connect with confidence.

Whether you experience mild apprehension or a paralyzing fear of networking, you're not alone. I too felt afraid. I'd walk into a networking event and slowly make my way toward the registration desk. Within seconds, my stomach would start to turn as I observed eager networkers writing names across name tags. The doors of freedom leading back to the parking lot called my name. Next, I'd awkwardly stand in line, secretly hoping an emcee would announce the gathering was canceled. The voices in my head screamed ugly things like *"Why are you here? You don't even know what you're doing!"* I could always count on my defeated self-talk or conscience to bark lies at me rapid-fire. Finally, I'd muster the courage to walk inside, get a drink, repeatedly check my watch, then search for the designated wallflower section to report for duty. Misery loves company.

Networks are powerful things, and in today's rapidly changing world, building and sustaining authentic relationships is more crucial than ever. Both traditional and social networks create exciting possibilities to network smarter, but only if you invest the time, patience, and perseverance necessary to reap the rewards. While there are many benefits to networking, it doesn't come easily for everyone.

You Have to Do the Work

There is no secret reveal in this chapter or even in this book. If you want something bad enough, commit to it, and do the work. This means accepting that in the networking process, you will sometimes fail. The key, however, is not to quit. There's a difference between quitting and failing. You must choose to risk failure in order to evolve and grow. Sadly, too many give up. While I consider myself a transformational networking coach, there's one service I will never be able to provide others. I will never be able to face, manage, or remove internal fears for you. I provide effective coaching tools and affirmations to help ease fear's sting, but facing what scares you, that's a solo sport.

@KariMirabal
There's a difference between
quitting and failing.

What Are You Afraid Of?

Countless professionals share their testimonies and networking fears with me. Some share they are afraid to talk to strangers while others fear getting stuck in an unfulfilling job. Regardless of what scares you, to overcome it you're going to have to face it.

We've Stopped Running from Saber-Toothed Tigers

When my youngest son was three, his older brother told him a local Mexican grill put grass in their rice (It was cilantro). I assured him it was just spice, not grass, but his brain played tricks on him and he continued to feel triggered when he looked at the rice.

Why do our brains play tricks on us when logic tells us otherwise?

Fear saved our ancestors from demise when running from saber-toothed tigers. It's how humans survived. Whether or not the danger you face is real or perceived, your body prepares you. When afraid, your body either fights or takes flight. We'll explore this topic further in this chapter.

@KariMirabal
Whether or not the danger you face is
real or perceived, your body prepares you.

What Vibes Are You Sending?

I believe we're always sending some type of vibe to the universe. Meaning, we are either attracting positive or negative energy based on our actions, words, and body language. For example, if you feel afraid of rejection at a networking event (cue slumped shoulders and no eye contact), you're projecting negative energy that most will translate as a "please don't talk to me" sign. Gloomy auras can make others feel uncomfortable and often translate to missed opportunities at networking events. Instead, turn a weakness into a strength by admitting to others how you're feeling. If you feel nervous talking to strangers, make your truth part of your introduction. "Hello, I'm Diane. This isn't easy for me because I'm nervous talking to new people, but may I join this conversation?" Most people will empathize and appreciate your display of courage and authenticity. Feeling nervous isn't a weakness if you lean into the vulnerability it creates. When you demonstrate strength by owning your insecurities, it often sets the stage for others to own and share their insecurities too.

Many cite fears of rejection as their number one barrier to networking. While rejection is par for the course in the art of connection, it can be a helpful, not hurtful, tool. Not everyone understands that networking is about developing mutually beneficial relationships. Those who reject your invitation to exchange information are more than likely not going to be "the right people" for you to network with anyway. You will naturally attract, or repel, different types of people as you exchange information with strangers. The trick to discerning who will be the right or the wrong type of contact to build in your network requires being brave enough to show others your true self. Don't be afraid to be vulnerable. When you display authenticity, you naturally attract the right people to or from your energy. I welcome rejection because, in the long run, it saves me time and energy. I prefer to invest my time, knowledge, and referrals with people who are open to reciprocating.

As you walk around a networking event, let your body language speak for you. Wear a smile and maintain eye contact to demonstrate confidence (even if it's not exactly how you feel inside). When others pick up your positive energy, they feel more at ease approaching you. It's these moments that increase your chance to make a powerful connection.

Networking isn't a perfect science, and that means the unexpected will happen. For instance, at one of my networking speaking engagements, my zipper broke as I was walking toward the stage. I spoke for the next hour with my left hand behind my back to keep my outfit from falling to the floor. My Naked Networking keynote would have had a totally different meaning that day. I kept my cool, projected confidence and delivered as promised.

Everyone Experiences Fear Differently

According to a study published in the *Washington Post*, public speaking is America's number one fear. While I do not possess that fear, I have different insecurities that make me feel afraid.

I fear I'm Not Enough.

In the process of writing this book, I experienced epic heartbreak. I was broken, confused, and lost for a bit. I prayed and begged God to "take the pain in my heart away." My fear of being alone after 20+-years of companionship absolutely terrified me. Yes, the confident woman on stage encouraging everyone to face their fear felt like a hypocrite. I spoke to audiences about overcoming networking fear, yet didn't have the courage to face my own insecurity. I felt embarrassed. During this trying season of my life, I realized running from pain versus facing it had become my habit. It was time to put on my BGPs (big girl panties). The universe invited me to be still. To face my fear and search for purpose inside the pain. What was the universe trying to teach me from this experience? What parts of me needed grace, compassion, and self-love? Why didn't I value myself enough to leave a hurtful relationship?

It was time to be strong and do the work.

She Meant Well

It was time to face my pain and explore the root of my fear. I can't ask audiences across the country and abroad to face their fear if I wasn't willing to face mine. Why did I think I was not enough? Why was I afraid of being single? Where did all this pain come from?

I grew up hearing conflicting messages regarding the definition of success. While my dad encouraged me to work towards my dreams, my mom believed a woman needed a man to survive. I was a spirited girl with an impatient spirit who pushed boundaries and spoke my truth. My mom wasn't shy to share her opinion as she groomed me based on her own beliefs and perspectives. She projected her fear that men wouldn't want someone like me because I thought and spoke independently.

I finally stopped resisting the pain. I knew the anguish would not diminish until it taught me what I needed to learn. I had to embrace those lonely nights and my misconception of failure. To process my fear, I needed help. I worked with a counselor to learn about letting go of "old stories" and started to rebuild my life. I focused on my sons, continued to participate in life groups through my church, attended women's retreats, set new dating boundaries, poured energy into my business, took a girls trip to Turks, and read about triggers, trauma bonds, and how the brain works in mysterious ways. I began to embrace the idea that being alone on a Friday night was far better than being with someone who didn't love the real me— flaws and all. I forgave myself. I forgave those who hurt me. Hurt people hurt people. I started to practice showing compassion to myself for the first time in my life. That's when things started to change.

YOU ALREADY HAVE THE NO

Something Small Invites Trouble

What do you fear most?

There are a myriad of fears and phobias. In my case, it was the imagined fear I wasn't enough. It's hard to believe something inside your brain called the amygdala—only about the size of an almond—can cause such strife.

When you think of the amygdala, think of one word–FEAR.

The amygdala wants to protect you so it's on the prowl for anything reminiscent of previous events that scared you. It recalls how you've historically responded to threats and, when unchecked, plays a central role in the way you emotionally respond. No matter how dangerous or innocent the object of your fear may be, when your amygdala senses danger, it makes a quick decision to launch the fight-or-flight response before your cortex (the part of your brain that controls logic) has time to overrule it. This cascade of events releases adrenaline, which may lead to increased heart rate, rapid breathing, a disconnect from rational thinking, and/or an inability to make good choices. When your amygdala's on high alert, your ability to speak eloquently is affected too.

Your amygdala heightens awareness to danger (whether real or imagined). It's the reason you feel afraid of things outside your control, like how strangers will react to you at a networking event. Feeling afraid can prevent you from meeting new people.

Don't Sabotage Yourself with Networking Lies

When delivering my keynote Naked Networking, I often ask audiences to raise their hands if networking is something they enjoy doing. Sadly, only about 10 percent of the people raise their hands. Why does networking get such a poor response? In most cases, people fear networking because of false stories—they've told themselves about the process of developing mutually beneficial relationships.

Don't sabotage your potential with networking lies. Instead, transform negative self-talk into powerful truth statements and you'll begin to shift your perspective. Overcoming networking fear takes practice but it can be done. A good place to start shifting perspective is the LTR (lies, truth, reframe) exercise I leverage in my Naked Networking coaching programs.

Below are examples of how the exercise works. Shifting perspective from a negative to a positive mindset can make a big difference in the way you approach networking.

The Naked Networking LTR Exercise (Lie, Truth, and Reframe)

Example One:

Step 1:
Identify a networking lie you've been telling yourself.

LIE:
Networking is only for people selling something.

Step 2:
Create a truth statement that contradicts the lie.

TRUTH:
Networking isn't synonymous with sales. It's about developing mutually beneficial relationships.

Step 3:
How can you view this networking challenge from a different perspective?

REFRAME:
Developing mutually beneficial relationships has the potential to yield business and personal benefits for me. Taking the risk to talk to a stranger might bring me closer to finding another like-minded person with whom I can exchange knowledge or enjoy activities. I ALREADY HAVE THE NO meaning: I'm already *not* on friendly terms with this new contact so what do I have to lose by inviting them to consider exchanging information with me?

Example Two:

LIE:
I'm a new software developer. I don't have anything of value to add to conversations here at the user group meeting.

TRUTH:
I'm feeling insecure around seasoned developers given my junior experience. I recognize I can bring fresh perspectives to the user challenge they are discussing because I was an end user not too long ago before I converted to development. I can be a contribution in a different way to this conversation.

REFRAME:
Everyone at this user group stood in my shoes as a beginner developer once too. If I am authentic and state my intention to learn as much as I can from their experience, I'm sure they will be open to including me. I ALREADY HAVE THE NO meaning: I'm already *not* included in their conversation, so sharing my intention to ask questions, learn, and grow

professionally might win me the opportunity to meet and exchange ideas with some great people. If I don't ask to participate, I won't learn anything new.

Example Three:

LIE:
I don't have time to network.

TRUTH:
I'm making up excuses again because I feel awkward talking to strangers.

REFRAME:
I waste 15 minutes about three times a day checking social media and playing games on my phone. If I decide to invest that time into connecting with new people on LinkedIn, I have the potential to add 2-5 new contacts to my existing network, which will grow in time if I do this one activity weekly.

What Lies Are You Telling Yourself?

Now it's your turn.

In the below space, work through the LTR exercise for yourself by documenting common lies you've been telling yourself about networking. Create a truth statement followed by a reframe statement to consider viewing each challenge from a different perspective. To get comfortable with the exercise, I recommend writing out each statement. With practice, you'll advance to taking the LTR exercise to a verbal stage where in the moment, you'll be able to interrupt negative thoughts and go through each step quickly to face your fear and network with confidence.

LIE:_____

TRUTH:_____

REFRAME:_____

LIE:_____

TRUTH:_____

REFRAME:_____

Afraid

LIE:_____

TRUTH:_____

REFRAME:_____

LIE:_____

TRUTH:_____

REFRAME:_____

LIE:_____

TRUTH:_____

REFRAME:_____

LIE:_____

TRUTH:_____

REFRAME:_____

Advanced Naked Networking LTR Exercise

By now you know that the muse of Naked Networking is developing mutually beneficial relationships. I'm inviting you to get naked (vulnerable) and start meeting new people with an honest and authentic approach. Networking is a process that requires courage, and that translates to experiencing the fear, risking rejection, and finding ways to process emotions that don't always feel great.

You can't control what happens to you, but you can decide not to let circumstances deflate you. In this chapter, you've learned how to identify a lie, create a truth statement, and the benefits of reframing negative self-talk. Now, I'm challenging you to take your LTR exercise to the next level by adding another statement to the process to help you recognize hidden potential inside every challenge you'll experience in the networking process.

Kyle Cease, transformation coach, author, and founder of Evolving Out Loud (www.kylecease.com), is a virtual mentor of mine. He first introduced me to the idea, and it has been an amazing tool in my networking journey. Cease suggests including the phrase "and I love that" whenever you experience a trigger. This process can help you explore new possibilities. It challenges you to stretch your thinking to include different ways to express, rather than repress, uncomfortable feelings.

Let's look at another example of an LTR exercise below. This time, add more to your truth statement by including an emotion you are feeling when triggered. With practice, you'll soon see for yourself how helpful this extra step in the networking LTR process can be. I call this advanced step the LTR + exercise.

69

LTR + Exercise

Example One

LIE:
Asking for a meeting with someone I just met is too bold.

TRUTH:
Asking for a meeting is just a request. I'm scared to feel rejected and I love that because feeling scared means I'm about to do something really brave.

REFRAME:
I'll go for it and ask for the meeting. I ALREADY HAVE THE NO meaning: I'm already *not* doing business with this contact so what do I have to lose if they say they are not interested in working with me? If this contact rejects my offer to meet, I'll find another contact with whom to work. There are many different doors inside this company, I'll find another entrance.

Example Two

LIE:
If I go to a networking event, I have to meet everyone who attends. That's too much pressure.

TRUTH:
I don't need to speak to everyone at every event. I'll focus on being selective. I want to focus on meeting the right people at the right time and the right place. I want to find people I can discuss issues that align with my workplace priorities. I'm feeling overwhelmed and I love that because feeling overwhelmed is an opportunity for me to learn to set boundaries.

REFRAME:

I will seek out networking events that gather healthcare industry professionals together. When I get there, I'll set a goal of meeting 2-5 new contacts versus worrying about working the room to collect as many business cards as possible. It's about quality, not quantity.

YOU ALREADY HAVE THE NO
Implementation

Have paralyzing fears kept you from achieving any of your dreams? Have they prevented you from going after career opportunities or affected your relationships? Many of us compensate and find coping strategies to work around fear because it just feels easier. However, facing fear makes you grow, so I'm daring you to evolve and step away from what's familiar. You'll rise when you work through fear and demonstrate a willingness to explore change. Acting despite fear will build confidence and test what you're really made of.

We all have things we're scared of, but in my experience, big risks often mean big rewards. I've made some huge leaps of faith in my life. Despite the butterflies in my stomach (a sign I'm on the right track), things typically work in my favor when I don't allow myself to think small. It's why I've dedicated the next portion of this chapter to sharing excerpts from my journey and three examples of how I made fear my bitch.

Are You Crazy? You're Pregnant.

I already considered myself a "success" when I stepped away from an IT recruiting leadership role with a Fortune 500 company nearly two decades ago. I made a six-figure salary, worked from a corner office in a beautiful Denver high rise, drove a fancy SUV, and led a team of amazing and talented employees. All of that changed in one minute's time. As I watched the pregnancy test reveal two red lines, I knew my career and life would never be the same.

What's your definition of success? Is it a C-level title, specific salary, or maybe a company you've always wanted to work for listed on your resume? Success means something different to everyone. To me, success meant being home to raise my boys yet finding a way to also maintain a career in the industry I loved: technology. I knew corporate America would never allow the lifestyle I wanted. I identified lies my ego wanted me to believe, then changed my focus to writing truth statements to balance the negativity. As a result, my best friend, JoAnn, and I decided to take the big leap. We began making plans to partner and launch an IT recruiting business. Comments like "are you crazy" and "you can't do this now, you're pregnant" streamed in daily. I focused on truth statements when triggered. JoAnn and I believed in our abilities and shared the same vision for our company. We named our S Corporation Clarity, Inc. Becoming a consultant was risky, but my desire to be a stay-at-home mom and raise my boys trumped fear. I was scared shitless, but I did it anyway. I wore yoga pants and baseball hats (go STL Cardinals) daily. We worked the phone and made sales calls to find clients relentlessly. I refused to let the idea of failure even enter my mind. To stay motivated, I merely had to look down and watch as my belly grew. We networked, took more calculated risks than ever before, and invested everything we made back into our business.

Making sales calls was tough but it was par for the course. When I felt discouraged, I reminded myself, YOU ALREADY HAVE THE NO. This meant telling myself again and again that I'm already *not* doing business with these contacts so what did I have to lose by going for the ask? If they said no, I would be in the exact same position I was before I made the call. I also knew there was a 50/50 chance these contacts would say yes.

JoAnn and I owned and operated Clarity, Inc. for the next eleven years. This business funded our dreams to stay home with our kids and maintain careers too. I joke that my oldest son Justus' first word was "Oracle" because he went with me to technology meetings where the only language spoken was pure geek. It was no surprise to me that Justus decided to study Information Technology in college. If you want something badly enough, face your fear. Find a way to make it work and don't give up before the miracle happens.

@KariMirabal
This is your life. If you believe in something,
don't let anyone take that away from you.

Job Board Post Turns Ugly

DICE is a website that helps IT professionals and hiring managers find each other. One day, I noticed an ad on their website featuring various IT men striking poses in their underwear. The campaign said "find the hottest tech talent." I thought the campaign was clever and shared it as a post from my profile on LinkedIn. Three hundred likes and 50-plus comments later, the jovial tone of social media took a different turn. Someone posted a comment on my feed inquiring why DICE didn't utilize women in this series of ads. It didn't take long to turn ugly. My post turned into a Kung Fu battle between IT men and women hurling less than professional digs back and forth.

These posts had me worried. I began telling myself lies. What if my clients saw this and didn't want to do business with me anymore? As I worked through the steps of identifying lies then writing truth statements, I felt tempted to take the easy way out and just delete the post. When I followed the steps and reframed the scenario, I reminded myself that social media is about engagement versus broadcasting. When I posted the ad, I created a space for others to share their opinions. It didn't mean I agreed with every comment posted, only that I hosted the discussion. Even though I felt afraid the negativity might go viral, I decided to keep the post active. I'm so glad I did because DICE saw my post and commented directly on the feed too. They invited both men and women IT professionals to audition for upcoming advertising campaigns right there on my post. The negative comments stopped almost immediately after. But this story isn't over yet. A few days later, I received a call from a DICE marketing manager who viewed my profile and asked me to participate in an interview about my business to be featured on their website. They noticed I helped recruit IT talent and believed my story aligned with their core blog themes. The piece they published included links to my website and information about my speaking topics and consulting services. I received awesome marketing exposure…and to think I almost deleted the post because I felt afraid.

@KariMirabal
Pause before you react to fear.
Is this real or perceived danger?

Networking at 38,000 Feet

Airplanes can be great places to meet new people. I first met Ben Whitesell on a flight back to Tulsa several years ago. It all started when I noticed the book he was reading, *Love*

Works: Seven Timeless Principles for Effective Leaders by Joel Manby. I thought to myself, YOU ALREADY HAVE THE NO—meaning, what did I have to lose by introducing myself and asking a few questions? I let my ego scare me a bit at first. It told me I was rude for interrupting someone I didn't know. Then, I told myself a truth statement and reframed the scenario. The worse that could happen would be Ben telling me he wasn't interested in further conversation. Nothing ventured, nothing gained, so I went for it and introduced myself. Lucky for me, Ben was open to conversation. Turns out we both worked in the technology industry, shared a passion for leading others, and had similar complaints about our kids. Ben, a talented project manager who worked for an established oil and gas company, inspired me. He unselfishly shared key takeaways from the book, which ignited further discussion. We learned through our talk that Ben registered to attend a project management conference where I was speaking a few weeks later. I admired Ben. He got on the plane and had a plan to read his book but instead chose to invest in communicating with a stranger. It ended up benefiting both of us. When the flight landed, he gave me his book, which is in my office library today. I was moved by his generosity. Ben and I have helped each other professionally time and time again since that day. I'm thankful Ben is in my network of leaders I turn to for advice and support. Building an arsenal of people takes time, dedicated effort, and a willingness to create—not wait—for opportunities.

Eating Crow Changed My Life

Networking has always been a critical component in IT recruiting. While working a project to find a software developer, I came across a situation that would set my amygdala into overdrive.

I received the name of a developer who worked for my client's competitor. We recruiters love referrals, so I jumped at the opportunity to introduce myself to him. I called the competitor and asked the receptionist to transfer me to Paul Jones, a seasoned software developer who had the skills my client wanted. In our business, if you're not a client, you're a source. I doodled impatiently on my paper as I waited for Paul to answer the phone. In the back of my mind, I started thinking, YOU ALREADY HAVE THE NO, meaning, I'm already *not* representing this candidate so what do I have to lose by going for it even though he is already employed? If he declines to work with me, I'm in the exact position I was before the call. I've lost nothing. However, if the candidate says yes, and there's a 50/50 chance he will, my client will be ecstatic.

Finally, I heard a voice. "This is Paul, can I help you?"

I had mastered the art of quick introductions by this time in my career. Most hiring authorities spend less than 15 seconds reviewing resumes so I knew I had even less time to make a powerful first impression on this call. Paul was quiet as I shared my intention for reaching out. I mentioned perks, salary range, cutting edge technology, and how the company allowed jeans on Fridays (yes, that used to be a thing). "Hello," I said. No response. "Excuse me ... Paul?" I said with an inquisitive tone. The silence was deafening. A stern voice said, "Do you know who you're talking to?" "Yes," I said, confidentially. "You're Paul Jones, a software developer with the exact programming experience my client seeks." "No" I heard him say. "I'm Paul Thomann, President of this company." In that moment, I realized the receptionist transferred me to the wrong Paul.

Amygdala Activated

I felt a rush of adrenaline. I felt afraid, and my heart started beating quickly. For half a second, I thought about hanging up, but I took a breather and decided to do what was right. I owned it and ate crow. I understood why Paul Thomann was heated, and invited him to hear me out. We talked about the current IT trends, emerging technologies, and how even the best recruiters could not recruit top talent from him if his employees feel appreciated and valued. Paul Thomann, President of the company, asked me to meet in-person to continue the conversation. I owed it to him and agreed.

To prepare for the meeting, I followed my steps and identified lies, created truth statements, and reframed the situation from a different perspective. I was prepared as Paul and I sat down to talk. Like a parent scolding a child for misbehavior, I expected to get an earful. However, my eyes popped out of my head when Paul offered me a job. He told me he wanted my type of aggressive approach for an upcoming project he and his team were having difficulty filling. I declined the full-time job, but proposed we explore a consulting partnership. Paul introduced JoAnn and I to other executive leaders within the company, and we signed a contract soon after. We ended up building and sustaining a partnership that lasted over eleven years. We continue to stay in touch with Paul and the other executives, but we no longer refer to them as partners; they became trusted friends.

@KariMirabal
Take the risk:
Let the YOU ALREADY HAVE THE NO mindset
lead you to new possibilities.

Build an Arsenal of People

Networking is about developing mutually beneficial relationships. Connections are valuable for many reasons:

career opportunities, meeting like-minded people, increasing sales, and even romance can spark from networking. The word networking should be written *netWORKing* because the act itself requires more work. Most want the benefits without investing the effort. You must build and sustain an arsenal of people to ask for support when the need(s) should arise. The challenge? You never know exactly when the person you meet today will help you succeed in the future. Patience is a virtue in the art of networking. I believe people fail at connection because they wait to network until it's too late. Panic leads to desperate places, and the frenzy you project to others doesn't translate well. Naked Networking is about recognizing and taking advantage of unique moments others often miss. Be an opportunist; work to build and sustain your network.

The Fight for Freedom

Once fear takes hold, walls start to build. Walls prevent you from moving forward in confidence and assurance. Let's not forget about fear's cousins: dread and worry. This entire group of emotions wreaks havoc on networking potential. Dread and worry start in your mind but affect your body too. They put stress on your entire system and sometimes cause headaches, muscle tension, and stomach problems—to name a few. Does any of this sound familiar?

Nelson Mandela said, "I never lose. I either win or learn." I couldn't agree more. If you're reading this book, you're interested in exploring what networking can do for you too. The YOU ALREADY HAVE THE NO mindset changed my thinking and helped me get comfortable taking new risks. Embrace the power of NO to empower yourself to push through, and not avoid fear.

Consider the Possibilities

Franklin D. Roosevelt said in his first inaugural speech, the "only thing we have to fear is fear itself." In the last chapter, Neglect, I challenged you to consider the downside of avoiding your network. When fear tempts you to leave networking to others, use the tools you've learned and never stop imagining the possibilities and opportunities available to you. The next time you walk into a room filled with strangers, get curious. Someone in the room might very well change your life. More importantly, you may change theirs for the better. When you view networking as an adventure versus a task, the magic begins to unfold.

I roll my eyes when motivational speakers say, "facing fear is a journey." Blah, blah. I disagree. Facing fear is a fight. A fight within yourself to take a good hard look at what scares you and why. The strongest weapon you have in this fight is your desire to reach your goal. When challenged, begin with the end in mind. What do you want? Why do you want it? Let that focus move you forward. Accept the unknown and practice the art of getting comfortable feeling uncomfortable. Push through pain—rewards are waiting on the other side of your fear.

Retraining your brain and pushing through fear versus running from it helps maintain your ongoing wellbeing. Fear-induced experiences don't have to create extreme stress in your life any longer.

What do you have to lose?

YOU
ALREADY
HAVE
THE
NO

Chapter 4 Key Takeaways

- YOU ALREADY HAVE THE NO–adopt the mindset and take the 50/50 risk.
- Quitting and failing aren't the same thing.
- Regardless of what scares you, face it to overcome it.
- Facing fear isn't a journey, it's a fight.
- Negative vibes make others feel uncomfortable and translate to missed opportunities for you.
- Building an arsenal of people takes time, dedicated effort, and a willingness to create—not wait—for opportunities.
- Add "and I love that because ..." when working through feelings that trigger you.
- Practice identifying Lies, Truths, and Reframing the situation from a different perspective.
- Naked Networking (vulnerability) requires courage and taking risks.

Chapter 5
Knowledge

"Opportunity dances with those on the dance floor."
- H. Jackson Brown, Jr.

The N.A.K.E.D. acronym represents five common networking barriers including **N**eglect, **A**fraid, **K**nowledge, **E**ngage and **D**edicate. In this chapter, we'll explore the barrier, **Knowledge.** You'll learn new strategies for networking with strangers and simple ways to connect with confidence. You have the will; now it's time to apply the right skill to get you where you want to go, faster.

Early in my career, I lacked both the desire and skill to network efficiently and effectively. Once I realized the value of networking, I discovered my will, but my skill was lackluster. Awkward handshakes, nervous smiles, and inauthentic conversations humiliated me. I remember times when I put my foot in my mouth as I talked to new people then walked away feeling embarrassed and defeated. In short, my networking was a mess. Luckily for me, failure has historically been my best instructor. I learned early on networking isn't a one-time event, it's a process. If you lack skill but have will, the three-step process outlined in this chapter, along with real-world examples, will help you gain the knowledge you need to build and sustain a powerful network.

Be Strong. Do the Work.

Networking is a gift that keeps on giving. It's important to stay committed through the entire process. Some connections will come easily, while others will require more work. Remember, setbacks are often setups for the universe's plan to steer you in different directions. Get curious and go with it to see where the path takes you. Some of my best networking connections are products of failure. I've been rejected more times than I can count, but I've learned those experiences often lead to better opportunities. No matter how long it takes to reach your networking goal, don't give up. Be strong and do the work.

Preparation Leads to Confidence

Preparation leads to confidence. The networking process increases your confidence and your chances to meet and exchange meaningful conversations with target audiences. To achieve success and stay your course, visualize beginning with the end in mind. Gain the most from networking events and time invested at conferences or corporate events by implementing the basic action steps below.

Networking Events, Conferences, Corporate Events

5 Action Steps

1. Review event website.
2. Identify contacts listed on event website.
3. Consider who you'd like to meet (i.e., leadership team, speakers, authors).
4. Log in to LinkedIn.
5. Make initial contact by sending a LinkedIn personal connection request.

Example—First Contact:

Hi Emma,

I see you will be speaking at the upcoming JuMar conference in St. Louis. I'm excited to attend this technology event and look forward to hearing your presentation. Thanks, Kari

Knowledge Tip:

Initial outreach only invites your target contact to connect. Wait for the second contact to share more details about your intention. Increase your chances to connect on LinkedIn by keeping things simple.

Example—Second Contact (after contact accepts your connection request):

Emma,

Thanks for accepting my connection request.

I'm looking forward to hearing your session on diverse AI technologies at the JuMar conference in St. Louis. I am new to AI and seek opportunities to learn from seasoned professionals like yourself to learn from at this event and beyond.

If there's anything I can do to be of assistance to you and your business, please don't hesitate to reach out.

Thanks,
Kari
karimirabal.com

Knowledge Tip:

With each contact made, increase the amount of information shared and always offer to help target contacts as well. Include your website or phone number each time from this point forward. Make it easier for the contact to reach you. These trust signals help establish rapport.

Example—Third Contact (ask for the meeting):

Hi Emma,

Hope things have been going well for you since we last connected. Looking forward to hearing your presentation at the upcoming JuMar conference.

Question…would you be open to meeting briefly during the conference?

My intention is to ask a few AI questions to gather your opinion about suggested certifications I'm interested in obtaining.

I noticed a networking break scheduled on 2.17 for conference participants at 3PM. Could we meet in the lobby during that break for 15 minutes?

Thanks for considering,

Kari
karimirabal.com

PS: I read STL weather will be beautiful that week. If time permits, I wanted to recommend exploring the new Gateway Arch Museum—a sight to see!

Knowledge Tip:

By the third contact, use a conversational tone and share your intentions.

Add personal points of interest, suggestions, links to more information, etc. Be an asset by sharing knowledge. Ask for a meeting and include specific dates/times. If your contact is unavailable at the time you propose, ask for alternative options from them. Contacts may propose a phone call or email QA exchange versus meeting in person, and that's perfectly fine. Chances improve to begin building authentic connections that are mutually beneficial with each contact made.

Not all target contacts will respond to networking requests favorably, but YOU ALREADY HAVE THE NO, so why not go for it and ask? You've nothing to lose. With each attempt, you practice your craft and polish your process. Learn from each experience and keep moving forward. You'll be surprised how one contact leads to another and another, and before you know it, you're networking with ease.

Be Different

Take a proactive approach to developing warm leads with target contacts before events even occur. When you do, you'll stand out in a crowd because you will be able to approach your target contact with a familiar tone due to previous correspondence. Those who don't take these steps risk introducing themselves for the first time at networking events and have to work harder to build a warm lead. Apply these steps and let them serve as a conduit for meaningful conversations. Those who network smarter know they must make the most of every opportunity that unfolds.

@KariMirabal
Use conversational tones when
building network contacts.

Don't Use Pliers to Drive a Nail

The dictionary defines a tool as "anything used as a means of accomplishing a task or purpose." You wouldn't use pliers to drive a nail. In the art of networking, the right tools can make or break you.

In the previous chapter, Afraid, I shared my fear of rejection and how it held me back from creating meaningful connections early in my career. I let fear feed me lies. One of my favorite lies was the idea that attending a networking event unprepared was fine. Networking was already uncomfortable, so I convinced myself that showing up and "winging it" was better than not going at all. No wonder my networking was such a disaster and didn't produce any fruit early in my career.

You never get a second chance to make a first impression so equip yourself with the right tools to achieve the best possible outcome. To increase your confidence and make authentic connections, fill your networking toolbox with must-have tools including a memorable tagline, a strong tell me about yourself statement, business cards, and real-world narratives that help new contacts understand how you've made impacts. Let's explore these must-have networking tools further. YOU ALREADY HAVE THE NO, so why not go for it and leverage new tools to help you make powerful impressions?

Four Must-have Networking Tools

A Memorable Tagline

A tagline is a phrase that you associate with your personal brand through repetition. This tool is helpful in the networking process for quick introductions. They are also used on business cards, LinkedIn headlines, resumes, and during interviews. Taglines communicate your passion and professional purpose. When I meet new contacts and they ask me what I do, my typical response is, "I teach people how to network smarter." Of course, they ask what that means, and I reply by telling them I travel the country and abroad speaking at conferences and corporate events sharing knowledge about how to authentically network. I also provide on-site masterclasses for companies who desire to have their employees learn how to network, as well as individual executive coaching services. Don't be boring by introducing yourself by name and official title only. Instead, meet new contacts with a sense of confidence by creating memorable taglines that pique curiosity and invite engagement for further conversation.

Tagline Examples:

"I help companies avoid legal disaster." - Lawyer

"I shift chaos into clarity to drive project success." - Project Manager

"I develop software that helps users work efficiently." - Software Engineer

"I'm your barber's barber." - Barber shop owner

"I lead teams that inspire positive change in the workplace." - Executive Leader

"I create unique marketing strategies designed to increase sales." - Sales

Tell Me About Yourself Statement (TMAY)

Invest time in creating a powerful tell me about yourself (TMAY) statement to use when meeting new people. Over time, there will be different versions of your TMAY for different times in your career. Your job interview TMAY will be different than your networking event TMAY, which will be shorter. Bottom line, your TMAY is your go to response to the question, "So, what do you do?"

It's a simple question that, unfortunately, few manage to answer well. Recognize the value a TMAY holds when sharing knowledge with others. It serves as a foundation for personal connections. Some complain they do not like the idea of a prepared TMAY statement because it comes across as inauthentic or robotic. In my experience, it's not the words you choose in your TMAY but the delivery of the TMAY that counts most. Develop a TMAY statement you like then practice, practice, practice, and then practice again. The more you practice, the easier it gets to deliver and the more professional you sound when sharing knowledge with new contacts. Reciprocation is very important in networking, so be sure to ask the other party to share what they do too before the conversation closes.

TMAY Statement Example:

"I work with people who feel uncomfortable talking to strangers. In short, I teach people how to network smarter. I do this work through a variety of channels including keynotes, masterclasses, and individual coaching programs designed to help people face fear so they can connect with confidence. What about you, what do you do?"

Business Cards

Business cards are an important tool in your networking toolbox. I am always baffled by people who tell me they forgot their cards or don't have one when meeting for the first time. It can create an awkward moment. The process of exchanging business cards is critical to networking success and helps drive positive first impressions. Business cards let people know who you are and how they can reach you. They pique curiosity and are great places to include your tagline for conversation starters. For example, my business card includes a photo on the back of me with my first microphone at the age of seven. Nine out of ten times, new contacts will make a comment about the picture and smile. I respond by sharing a quick story about how my passion for public speaking started at a young age. Mixing business with personal information helps make memorable conversations during business card exchanges.

Always Carry

You never know when opportunities will present themselves. Carry business cards in your purse or wallet at all times. You just never know when or where you'll meet someone. Everyone needs business cards, whether you are employed or not. If you are currently working, carry both corporate and personal business cards. If you meet someone interested in contacting you for a new career opportunity, you wouldn't want them contacting you at work, so make personal business cards for those scenarios. I've heard horror stories over the years about companies discovering their employees used work hours and resources to converse with competitors. Play it safe.

When designing your business card, keep it simple. Include name, email, contact number, and tagline.

@KariMirabal
When designing business cards, keep it simple.

The following is a sample business card:

BETSY COX
software developer

I Help Streamline End User Productivity & Profitability

+1 (954) 343-0061
betsy@betsycox.com
betsycox.com

What - How - Result (WHR) Stories

Sharing stories helps make memorable experiences when meeting new people. Stories convey your purpose and passion. As you describe the story, the person you're talking to runs a visual through their mind imagining pictures that match your narrative. Equip yourself with impactful What, How, Result (WHR) stories and leave lasting impressions. The simple WHR format provides a template to follow as you share knowledge with others.

The below WHR template helps you stay organized and limits excessive babble that can eat precious time when exchanging information. Ideally, you want each WHR story to be under two minutes.

What: Did you do?

How: Did you do it?

Results: Explain why your contributions made a difference.

90

Create A "Me-File"

Drawing a blank for story content? Start now to create a "Me—File" that's only purpose is to track notes related to achievements that might one day be share-worthy: projects you've completed, promotions earned, training or certifications, lessons learned from work experiences, leadership tips, any professional success that was a direct result of your actions, etc. Your "Me-File" serves as a reminder before attending networking events to jog your memory for conversation starters to potentially share. If you attend an IT conference for example, look to your "Me-File" for specific stories related to technology projects you're working on now or in the past. Choose a story from your "Me-File" arsenal that relates to the contact with whom you're talking.

WHR Example:

What:
What I want to share is how I teach people how to network smarter.

How:
How I do this is through keynotes, masterclasses, and individual coaching.

Result:
The results of my work help people face fear so they can connect with confidence.

When sharing your story, specifically use the three words (What, How, and Results) as your story unfolds. It helps frame the information in bite-sized pieces so the person you are talking to can follow the story better. Framing your stories in this format also keeps time from escaping you. Target each WHR story to last between 30-60 seconds.

@KariMirabal
WHR stories set you apart from the competition.

The 3-Step Networking Strategy

When I embraced the power of networking, the will needed to talk to strangers took care of itself, but I still lacked the skill. If you have the desire to network but want a proven process to help you make lasting impressions, this 3-step networking process is proven and will help you build outstanding networks. The 3-step networking process includes Plan, Connect, and Grow. I love this strategy because it works for both traditional and social media networking. When you implement the plan, connect, and grow strategy, watch what happens as you let each step guide your process and bring you closer to your networking goals. Let's take a closer look at each step and how each helps you build and sustain powerful networks.

Step One: Plan

The best question to ask yourself as you begin the planning step is, who do you want to talk to and why? While a large percentage of my clients is in the technology industry (a large group of people who historically dislike talking to strangers), I have found sticking to a solid plan helped them minimize anxiety concerning networking. People often think extroverts have the advantage over introverts, but that is not true. Both personality types can be successful at networking. Extroverts tend to feel more comfortable talking to strangers initially, but introverts are better listeners.

To maximize your networking effort, plan ahead by considering who your target audience is and what your best possible outcome might be. Begin researching your target contact's background, education, personality traits and career experience. Take notes as you research. LinkedIn is a great social media platform to support these efforts, as are other social media sites and the web in general. Preparing by planning who you want to talk to and why provides a roadmap or sense of direction to make you feel more comfortable.

@KariMirabal
Conduct research on target contacts to explore potential commonality.

Planning helps when nerves kick in. When you exchange information with new contacts, you'll thank yourself later for the time you invested to learn more about each person. This step not only keeps you organized, but also leaves a strong first impression regarding your competence and your confidence. Something as simple as a spreadsheet format (example below) or a CRM (customer relationship management) tool help you stay organized. You just need a central place to document contact information and notes to jog your memory about each potential contact. When your new connection contacts you, use this information to recall commonality or details that will demonstrate to your contact that you've done your homework.

PLAN	NOTES	CONNECT	NOTES	GROW	NOTES
Aaron Nicholson	IT Project Manager with WCD Energy in St. Louis, MO. BPO: Exchange info about ERP systems (recommended products, prices, efficiency, etc.)				

Example of spreadsheet notes

93

Step Two: Connect

As you progress to step two, connect, consider which channel might be the best to reach your target contact. If you want to network with a 73-year-old CEO of a manufacturing company, Snapchat will likely not be your best connection channel. Instead, consider which path will yield a higher probability of receiving a response and select that road. In the example of the 73-year-old CEO, consider a "snail mail" introduction letter, a phone call, customized email, or request a personal introduction from a mutual contact.

When it comes to the connection portion of the three-step process, mix your media with each attempt to reach new people. If your first connection attempt does not return a response, try again using a different media channel. If you sent an email the first time, reach out by phone the next. Leave detailed voicemails as needed and be sure to share your intention, smile through the phone, and politely request 15 minutes of their time to exchange information. If your second attempt does not produce a response, send a personalized letter through the post office (or drop one off with the receptionist with your business card inside the envelope) for a third attempt.

@KariMirabal
Choose appropriate channels to reach your target contact or risk losing any chance of connecting.

Target contacts are busy. Give potential network connections time to get back to you between each outreach action (3-5 days between each). Log each activity in your spreadsheet or CRM to help you track your actions, dates, and personal notes for each network contact along the way to stay organized.

94

PLAN	NOTES	CONNECT	NOTES	GROW	NOTES
Aaron Nicholson	IT Project Manager with WCD Energy in St. Louis, MO. BPO: Exchange info about ERP systems (recommended products, prices, efficiency, etc.)	Sent LinkedIn connection request on 02.17.19 with mention of our mutual contact, Mike Page from InfoMart.	Reach out again 2.25.19 if no response.		

Example of spreadsheet used to track process

Step Three: Grow

Most people have experienced the stab of fair-weather friends—people who pop in and out of your life only when they want something. Networking means developing mutually beneficial relationships. Grow, the third step, helps you continue to stay in touch with target contacts. Of all the steps, the grow step seems to be the one that challenges most people. Who has time to stay in touch daily with every contact in your network? Thankfully, social media can help. Stay on your network's radar at the same time you establish yourself as a subject matter expert by posting content that adds value to others. Choose relatable articles to share, post new career opportunities or corporate updates, offer leadership or industry book suggestions, upload favorite quotes or simply share a TED or TEDx Talk you believe to be beneficial. Post appropriate content accordingly per social site you select. For example, on Twitter, it is not uncommon to tweet up to 20 times a day but on LinkedIn, I don't recommend posting beyond three to five times a week.

@KariMirabal
Leverage social media to share content and offer value to your network.

When potential networking opportunities arise, don't miss them. Use the YOU ALREADY HAVE THE NO approach to challenge yourself to take new risks. The benefit of seeing new jobs or potential client leads first is valuable. Most of these occur through the referral pipeline. Time kills deals so strike while the iron is hot. For example, if you see someone in your network posted an inquiry asking for a service or contact but you wait three to five days to respond, it may already be too late. Another example, when you observe a new job posting, pause before you pass and consider who in your network might benefit from knowing about this opportunity. When you share information with others—information that doesn't immediately benefit you—your value rises within your network. Building powerful networks is only half the battle. Growing your network through continued communication and being a contribution to those who trust you makes all the difference in the world to your networking results.

PLAN	NOTES	CONNECT	NOTES	GROW	NOTES
Aaron Nicholson	IT Project Manager with WCD Energy in St. Louis, MO. BPO: Exchange info about ERP systems (recommended products, prices, efficiency, etc.)	Sent LinkedIn connection request on 02.17.19 with mention of our mutual contact, Mike Page from InfoMart.	Reach out again 2.25.19 if no response.	Sent Aaron an invite to the upcoming Chamber Networking event on 07.15.19. Sent link and mentioned free ticket if he meets me there.	Ask Aaron if he knows anyone over at American Airlines in the operations department for potential leadership masterclass opportunities.

Example of spreadsheet used to organize your process

Plan, Connect, and Grow Recap

Consistency is king when using the Plan, Connect, and Grow strategy. Always know which step you are on with each contact to help you keep a steady pace for follow up. Ask yourself which of the three steps could use more work and why. Focus your efforts on equally allocating time and activity

YOU ALREADY HAVE THE NO

for each step to gain optimal returns. For example, I've seen clients spend too much time planning and not enough connecting, or they plan and connect with no problem, but then disregard the grow step to maintain the relationship.

@KariMirabal
Which of the three networking steps
challenges you the most and why?

Real-World Examples

3-Step Networking Strategy

I've leveraged the 3-step networking strategy, Plan, Connect, and Grow, for years in the real-world and my personal life. I'm always amazed at the generosity of people and how simply asking for help creates opportunities to authentically connect. THE YOU ALREADY HAVE THE NO, so-why-not-take- the-risk approach, led me to some pretty awesome breakthroughs. The following are some examples of my success stories to inspire creative thinking and pique your curiosity about what results you too can achieve using this strategy.

Who Viewed My Profile

Plan:

I utilize the LinkedIn feature "who viewed my profile" and check it daily. I noticed the CIO of a very large healthcare company, Wheeler Coleman, viewed my profile. This piqued my curiosity and I did some research. What a great potential network contact to explore given our technology backgrounds.

97

Connect:

I chose to connect by LinkedIn. I knew he was active on the platform and in my initial connection message, I asked if he had any questions because I noticed he had viewed my profile earlier that week. First, I offered help. He responded with questions about networking which led to multiple exchanges and an eventual discovery phone call. I found Wheeler to be a forward-thinking leader who I believed I would learn many things from. When he invited me to Chicago to develop strategies together, I jumped at the opportunity. There was only one caveat, I wouldn't go to a Cubs game—unless they were playing the Cardinals (LOL). We agreed to go to a White Sox game and a mutually beneficial business relationship began. Since that initial connection, I've continued to support a variety of Wheeler's employees with networking and career development coaching programs.

Grow:

Long after our first project came to a close, Wheeler and I continued to grow our networking relationship through referrals and by simply staying in touch. Don't be a fair-weather friend. Plan, connect, and then continue to grow your mutually beneficial relationships. I had a 50/50 chance of working with Wheeler when I applied the YOU ALREADY HAVE THE NO approach. I figured I already *wasn't* doing business with his company so what did I have to lose if he said no? Taking the risk paid off. Although we started working together when he was a healthcare executive, we each evolved over time. Wheeler is now the CEO of EC-United, a boutique executive consulting firm headquartered in Chicago. They provide clients with cyber security assessments, performance management, interim leadership, and emerging technology solutions. When Wheeler launched his company, he continued to have me to train his new hires.

Politics and the Police

Plan:

First 48, a television show filmed in various cities in the United States, offers an insider's look at the real-life world of homicide investigators. I was proud to see the Tulsa Police Department included. I felt a sense of pride when I witnessed these officers keeping our communities safe and jotted down their names. I planned to reach out to them in appreciation for their service.

Connect:

I chose to connect by phone to some of the officers and extend my gratitude for their work. In my connection outreach, I offered to help these officers, their families, and/or anyone in their network as a thank you for their sacrifices. It was during this exchange I met Luke Sherman. Luke is a decorated 20+ year veteran with the Tulsa Police Department, a Sergeant over the Tulsa Fugitive Unit, respected chairman with the National Tactical Officers Association (NTOA), and the owner of Aegis CPG, a growing Tulsa based security consulting company. He returned my call and thanked me for the kind words. It was at that time he mentioned running for Tulsa County Sheriff and invited me to meet for lunch to take me up on my offer to support questions regarding networking. We met to discuss his questions and how he could incorporate more social media platforms into his political campaign. I was happy to share strategies and ideas to help him reach this goal. It was the first time I ever worked with someone running for a political office, and I knew I would learn so much.

Grow:

We continued to stay in touch over the years as we grew our networks. Luke had questions related to social media and networking, and ways he wanted to try and bring my networking topics into the Tulsa Police Department. Sometimes I had questions concerning my teenage boys—stories not included in this book (smile). Together we've built and continued to experience a mutually beneficial relationship.

Duke University Lacrosse

Plan:

My oldest son wanted to play lacrosse for Duke University but his grades were not so great. I spoke to him often about the importance of applying himself at school, but I sounded like a broken record. I knew I wasn't making any headway (what do moms know anyway?). My plan was to find someone to whom my son would listen. It didn't matter to me who delivered the message, as long as the message was received.

Connect:

I chose to connect by LinkedIn. I located a young man attending Duke University on LinkedIn. At the time, he was the captain of the Duke lacrosse team. He was also on the honor roll. I reached out to him and shared my challenges with my son. I asked if he would be open to encouraging my son with his college story. I hoped this idea would motivate him. The Duke student agreed and sent my son a package a few weeks later. In the box, he included a letter explaining how an athlete's career can be over in one injury, but no one can take education away. He outlined the responsibility of being on the lacrosse team and how if a top player's grades fell, those athletes risked being ineligible for games. When that happens, the entire team suffers. Bottom line, schoolwork is a priority. Included in the package was an autographed poster of the Duke lacrosse team. He was so excited. He framed the poster and it still hangs in his room today.

Grow:

This young man graduated from Duke University and we continued to stay in touch. I provide him updates about my son and offered my services to him. His encouraging words and acts of kindness helped my son break poor study habits and increase his morale. My son graduated high school with all As and Bs. He also learned a valuable lesson in the power of networking.

Egg on Face

Plan:

One day, I noticed the same guy had been reviewing my profile week after week on LinkedIn. His name was Tim Gorman. He was the Division Vice President of Rogers Group Inc., a construction company in a nearby state. I was curious why he returned week after week to view my profile, but I never received a call, connection request, or email from him. I decided to explore this story further. My ego and I wanted to know why he was "stalking" me.

Connect:

I chose to connect on LinkedIn. In my initial connection request, I asked if there was anything I could help him with since he kept viewing my profile. Yes, this was a wee bit snarky in tone. I wasn't as humble then as I am now. I'll never forget how Tim responded with such grace to my inquiry. He complimented me on the fact that I published a leadership blog weekly. Tim shared that each week, he viewed my profile to read my leadership blog. He told me he used the diverse topics as discussion points at his weekly sales meetings. As I read his kind and gracious message where he complimented my blog and shared how he loved some of my leadership ideas, my mouth hung open and my cheeks turned pink. I remember grabbing an imaginary egg and cracking it on my face. What a fool I had been. Tim forever changed my perspective, and I never viewed anyone looking at my profile multiple times as a "stalker" ever again.

Grow:

Networking can teach us many lessons. I learned not to judge a book by its cover and to ask questions before making assumptions. I thanked Tim for his kind words. I applied the YOU ALREADY HAVE THE NO approach and invited him to engage with me in ongoing dialogue around which topics he liked, didn't like, and why. I realized I wanted to go after a mutually beneficial relationship—there was nothing to lose by asking at that point. Tim graciously agreed. We began exchanging messages and talking about blogs that offered team building examples, like the Marshmallow Challenge originally developed by Peter Skillman, as well as blogs I missed the mark on from his perspective. I appreciated Tim's honest feedback. He became my informal blog reviewer. My writing skills evolved as a result of our business relationship. I wanted to deliver better blogs because I knew how he was leveraging them with his team. I've never met Tim in person, but we stay in touch often. He is a kind, generous, honest, and gracious human being. I am thankful not only for knowing him, but also for learning such a valuable lesson about myself in our experience. Truth be told, I didn't have the courage to tell Tim the true story about the days I thought he was a "stalker" until I started putting this book together and knew our story had to be part of it. Lucky for me, he laughed and allowed me to use his real name in the book.

You're Never Too Old (or Too Young) To Network Smarter

I began sharing networking knowledge with my boys at an early age. When my youngest son was nine, he received a baseball hat from the LA Dodgers signed by Magic Johnson. A mutual connection arranged this wonderful gift after she heard my son say the Dodgers were his favorite baseball team. I helped my son write a thank you note to Magic and leveraged the opportunity to explain networking basics. He pulled out his crayons and thanked Magic for the gift, included a picture with the hat, and went for the ask. He shared how he wanted to play baseball for the Dodgers one day. To this day, Magic continues to inquire about my son's baseball progress through our mutual connection and I am not shy about sharing his achievements to keep the lines of communication open (#ProudMom). Now in high school, my son plays baseball for one of the top organizations in the state of Oklahoma. His hat hangs in his room and serves as a reminder of his career goal. It also serves as a reminder that YOU ALREADY HAVE THE NO, so take the risk and see where it takes you. It's my hope both of my sons continue to apply their networking knowledge to develop mutually beneficial relationships throughout life.

Networking Is an Adventure

I once hated networking. Now I love it. It changed my life and the lives of many of my clients, family members, and friends. While it wasn't always easy, equipping myself with networking knowledge helped me push through barriers to experience the benefits. I am often asked how I maintain a positive attitude during the ebbs and flows of networking. To me, it is simple. Networking is an adventure. When I walk into a room full of new contacts, several thoughts go through my head. The first is always who can I help in this room, and the second is, who in this room might change my life. I look at each contact I meet as an opportunity. I never know how the story will end, but I am oh so curious to explore the possibilities. Taking new chances and helping more people keeps me engaged in the adventure.

What do you have to lose?

**YOU
ALREADY
HAVE
THE
NO**

Chapter 5 Key Takeaways

- YOU ALREADY HAVE THE NO—adopt the mindset and take the 50/50 risk.
- Preparation leads to confidence.
- When connecting with new contacts on LinkedIn, invite, thank the connection for accepting the request, and share your intention for reaching out.
- Create a way that works for you to organize networking activity.
- Keep a "Me-File" to document skills, training, accomplishments, certifications, examples of success and failure and anything notable that relates to your career. Reference this information when you need it to build a resume, recall during networking events, interviews, or during meetings with new connections.
- A powerful TMAY (tell me about yourself) statement helps you introduce yourself with confidence.
- Taglines are a fun way to communicate your business intention and make a powerful first impression.
- When sharing information, use the What, How, Result method to stay organized when communicating with others.
- Consider networking an adventure! Be open to where each connection can take you.
- Use the 3-step networking strategy to build powerful connections.

Chapter 6
Engage

"Opportunity dances with those on the dance floor."
- Anonymous

The N.A.K.E.D. acronym represents **N**eglect, **A**fraid, **K**nowledge, **E**ngage and **D**edicate. In this chapter, we'll explore the barrier, **Engage.** You'll learn common mistakes people make when approaching strangers and positive ways to engage others authentically when networking.

Walking into a room full of strangers can be an intimidating but necessary step to growing your network. Learning how to engage others while circulating within new crowds is an art that requires subtle skill. Networking isn't about gathering as many business cards as you can, it's about developing mutually beneficial relationships. In short, what can you do to help others? To engage others authentically, treat people as you want to be treated. Sounds simple, but approaching and maintaining conversations with strangers can feel overwhelming.

@KariMirabal
Circulating among crowds to network
is an art that requires subtle skill.

Networking Isn't Synonymous with Sales

I'm always surprised at the number of people who believe networking is only for sales professionals. Networking is not synonymous with sales. Networking is a life skill, one that can benefit everyone regardless of industry or title. You're never too young or too old to start developing mutually beneficial relationships. In the previous chapter, we explored knowledge and you learned about the 3-step networking strategy of Plan, Connect, and Grow. This method works well for both social media and traditional networking.

My children have been learning how to network smarter since they were little. My son learned more about networking when we were able to help his friend after he suffered third-degree burns from a fireworks explosion. While in the hospital, his friend went through physical and emotional pain, and we wanted to do something to help lift his spirits. This was a perfect opportunity to demonstrate how networking works. My son pointed out how much his friend loved a certain brand of athletic clothing. We discussed the 3-step strategy and came up with a plan. We began researching potential contacts within the athletic apparel company and reached out to their executives in hopes of getting their attention. Next, we explored the step connect. Within 48 hours, one of the company's senior leaders called us and asked how they could help his friend. The company sent my son's teammate a box of superhero clothing designs along with an autographed baseball bat from Bryce Harper of the Washington Nationals. This act of kindness helped lift the boy's spirits while he recovered from his injuries. Finally, I explained the grow step, where we reached out in appreciation to all the people who helped, and we discussed the importance of keeping in touch. Through these channels, I met some amazing people. After learning about my work, many had me help them update their company LinkedIn profiles. It was during this entire project that I first explained to my son the YOU ALREADY HAVE THE NO approach. What did we have to lose by asking this company for help? If the company said no, we were in the same position we were before we made any contact, so why not take the risk and go for it? We are thankful the company stepped up to the plate to help, thankful my son's friend recovered from his injuries, and thankful my son witnessed firsthand the power of connection.

@KariMirabal
Share networking intentions upfront.

Good, Bad, and Ugly Networkers

I've learned networking is a gift that keeps on giving once you've mastered how to connect authentically. Networking can be life changing. I know this from personal experience. You won't regret investing time in meeting and exchanging information with those who value developing mutually beneficial relationships. In the art of networking, I've witnessed the good, the bad, and the ugly. Let's explore each type, what to avoid, and how to overcome the barrier of engaging others.

Good

The good category of networkers includes those who truly relish connecting with people and supporting others. They don't give to get, they give to give. Good networkers appear to have a natural cadence; their process isn't forced. For them, it's a habit, and they seem to like the process. These are the people we admire for their natural ability to connect authentically. They appreciate the benefits of networking and don't take advantage of trusted circles. They're always willing to assist and lead by demonstrating.

Bad

The bad category of networkers includes those who mean well but lack authentic engagement mindsets. This category of people tends to give to get. They are willing to give the gift of helping, but they have expectations of reciprocating measures. If you give someone a gift laced with assumptions, is it really a gift? Probably not. Bad networkers participate at events out of obligation versus a burning passion for being a contribution to others. I hate to admit it, but most people fall into this category. They have the will and good intentions but don't fully commit, and thereby miss opportunities great networkers would identify. The good news is networking is a skill that can be learned. With patience, persistence, and practice, you can advance from a bad to a good networker.

Ugly

The ugly category of networkers includes people who are only out for themselves. They take from others and don't ever give back. Avoid these "slime" types at all costs.

@KariMirabal
Avoid slime approaches that
risk turning new contacts off.

Real-World Examples of Slime

Ever been a victim of a slimy approach disguised as networking? We all know the story. Slimy types pitch products and services without first building trust signals. Don't throw slime at people and expect them to want to network with you. If you're unsure if your actions are slimy or not, consider the similarities between networking and dating. A courting process in dating establishes rapport as people get to know each other. Let's look at a few examples of slime approaches and consider where things took a wrong turn. What could each person in the scenarios below have done differently to foster authentic engagement?

TEDx Talk: Career Dating

I received an email that included compliments about my TEDx Talk: Career Dating. This contact told me the video "inspired him and helped his career." Wondering why this compliment made it to the slime example section of this book? The words seem sincere except for the fact that my TEDx Talk on how to fall in love with your career again and again had not been published at the time I received his email. Slimy alert. I returned the correspondence inquiring how he gained special access to the TEDx video since it had yet to be published. Naturally, I did not receive a response, but I do hope the contact got the message. Authenticity in the engagement process is important.

What could this contact have done differently to foster authentic engagement?

Don't Call Me Lynn

I received correspondence from someone who said they "reviewed my website and thought I would benefit from their career coaching services." Interesting! I've been in the career coaching and recruiting business for the last 20 years, so it didn't really appear they had reviewed my website. To make matters worse, they used a canned template with the wrong name. In short, I was referred to as Lynn—twice. Now I make it a habit to give people the benefit of the doubt, so I thought perhaps they sent the message in error. I wrote back and expressed concern that the message came to the wrong contact, after all, I'm not Lynn. They wrote back that the message was for me, they just made a typo. Slimy alert. I explained I teach people how to network smarter and I wanted them to have more success in their business. I offered a consultation, pro bono, to discuss ideas around the best practices for authentic engagement. As you can imagine, they did not appreciate my offer and declined. When engaging others, take your time. Don't risk losing potential clients due to carelessness.

What could this company have done differently to foster authentic engagement?

@KariMirabal
Don't call me Lynn.

LinkedIn's not Match.com

A man I'd never met reached out to me on LinkedIn. He wanted to know if I would be interested in being his life partner because he liked my photos and the spirit of my personality. Really? Again, I give people the benefit of the doubt. After I rolled my eyes at this bizarre request, I wrote back with a spirit of grace telling myself he was just new to social media and confused about LinkedIn general etiquette. I mentioned if he were my career coaching client, I would counsel him that LinkedIn is a networking platform, not a dating site. I proceeded to recommend sites designed for romantic intentions such as eHarmony or Match.com. To my horror, he learned nothing from my correspondence because his return message asked if I had any friends who might be interested.

Romantic sparks can fly anytime, anywhere, and sometimes in the least expected places. However, you don't go to Home Depot to buy bread. There's a time and a place for everything, including romance. Don't risk turning others off with inappropriate use of platforms designed to develop mutually beneficial relationships.

What could this guy have done differently to foster authentic engagement?

@KariMirabal
Keep it professional. Use the right channels
to communicate the right message.

Teach People How to Treat You

Don't allow insincere people to waste your time with unintentional conversation at networking events. It's happened to me; it'll happen to you too. It represents everything wrong with how some people network. These negative types pretend they're listening, yet their eyes drift away as they scan the room for their next victim. Ever heard the saying, "a wise person once said nothing?" Let actions speak louder than words to teach people how to treat you. While attempting to hold a conversation with a new contact who isn't maintaining eye contact, try this strategy. Stop speaking mid-sentence when a contact's eyes veer off. When eye contact returns, resume your sentence. If their eyes begin to wander again, repeat the process. Continue these steps until they get the point or close the conversation and walk away. It's disrespectful. Invest time and energy into people who are interested in engaging you respectfully through active listening.

@KariMirabal
Always maintain eye contact.

How to Engage Others

We've examined three networking types, examples of what to avoid, and slimy approaches. Now, let's explore positive ways to respectfully and sincerely engage others in the networking process.

Increase Your Networking Engagement Strategy

- Wear a name tag
- Smile
- Shake hands
- Maintain eye contact
- Actively listen
- Reference contact's name
- Repeat main points shared
- Ask open ended questions
- Offer business cards, ask for theirs
- Thank contacts for their time
- Excuse yourself politely from conversations ("Great to meet you, I look forward to following up soon.")

Transform Weakness into Strength

If you've ever been nervous talking to strangers (hands shake, mouth gets dry, you feel like you're stumbling over your words), you're not alone. This is how it feels to be naked in the networking process. I've learned to address the elephant in the room directly to shift a weakness into a strength. If you're feeling nervous or want to recover from something you

114

said that didn't come out right, breathe. It happens to the best of us. Awkward moments can easily transform into engagement opportunities. When we admit we are feeling a bit nervous, most will empathize and offer words of comfort. If they know you are new to networking, chances are, they will help you carry the conversation and ask questions to ease your nerves.

Consider using these phrases to demonstrate vulnerability and to break conversation tension when talking to strangers.

- Apologies, I'm so nervous. Networking is new to me.
- Apologies, I'm a bit nervous. I'm not so good at networking yet.
- I apologize, I am a bit nervous. I'm still learning how to talk to new people.
- Thanks for being kind. This is my first networking event, I'm a bit nervous.

Break Ice Before Business

Following up and meeting with new contacts after events or introductions are the next steps in the networking process. I believe commonality leads to likeability between two people. Once you have likeability with someone, trust begins to grow. When trust is present between two individuals, opportunities for organic business conversation often emerge. To engage others authentically, do your research before each meeting. Break a little ice before you start talking business. Tap into commonalities to authentically engage with new contacts.

@KariMirabal
Commonality leads to likeability.

Finding commonalities before jumping into work topics generates camaraderie. For example, leverage social media to explore interests, education, and company background. Common interests may include being from the same hometown, participating in sports or being a fan of a certain team, books, leadership trends, and community interests. The YOU ALREADY HAVE THE NO approach helped you secure the meeting, now lean into commonalities to increase the probability of engagement. Commonalities discussed also serve as great topics for the follow-up. Tools like LinkedIn offer users opportunities to research shared interests. As you read through someone's profile, look for clues to what they enjoy doing outside of work. On my profile, I share my love of baseball (go St. Louis Cardinals), salsa dancing, and Star Wars. You'd be surprised how often these topics come up in random discussions. I look for things I have in common with each new contact and bring those items up when we meet or during follow up conversations. Have fun getting to know new people, and in the process, allow yourself to enjoy the experience of exchanging work and personal information. Breaking ice before business helps you authentically engage with others.

Keep It Open

To engage others and encourage more than a yes or no answer in return, keep conversations flowing by asking open-ended questions. Here are some of my favorite networking event questions. When meeting strangers for the first time at conferences, networking events, or corporate activities, use a combination of these phrases as you enter new conversations.

- How did you find out about today's event?
- What inspired you come to today's event?
- What do you think about the event so far?

116

- Which breakout session or track have you enjoyed so far?
- What new things are happening in your industry these days?
- What's your biggest challenge at work currently?
- How can I be helpful to you right now?
- Who would be a good prospect for you so I can keep my ear to the ground?
- What's your best possible outcome from today's conference?

@KariMirabal
To encourage continued conversation,
ask open ended questions.

Stick with Light Topics

When making small talk at networking events, avoid confrontational subjects including politics, religion, or topics that divulge too many intimate details about your personal life. Be engaging, be informed, and be a good listener in order to encourage engagement with others. If business opportunities are ahead, they will come up naturally in conversation.

Tone

Sometimes it's not what we say, it's how we say it that matters most when exchanging information with others. Regardless of the content of the things you say, it's your tone that communicates what you're feeling. Tone tells the truth even when our words don't. Often, it's your tone that prompts responses in others. Most of the time I advise people not to make assumptions when networking, but with tone, typically what you think you hear in another person's tone is almost always correct. However, tone works both ways when networking. If someone responds to you negatively, rather than getting defensive, pause for a moment to reflect on how your tone might have caused a reaction from someone else. Sure, it's easier said than done, but is worth noting as you evolve your networking skills.

Don't Judge a Book by Its Cover

When it comes to selecting potential networking contacts, don't judge a book by its cover. Many of my success stories stem from connections networkers who are inexperienced might have overlooked. One example is stay-at-home parents. While some might wonder what someone who doesn't work outside the home could do for someone who does, I encourage you to think again. Some families make the decision for one parent to stay home and they budget accordingly. Networking with the parent who stays home opens doors with the other parent too. It's like feeding two birds with one seed. I once networked with a woman whose husband was a doctor. That relationship led to other introductions, and I ended up conducting networking training classes at a large hospital. In short, don't assume anything, and treat everyone you meet as a golden potential networking contact.

Another example: Aaron, our pool service technician, overheard me one afternoon on a call exchanging information with a client. My client had been laid off from a Fortune 500 home improvement retailer. As Aaron cleaned the pool, he shared with me what a small world it was. He provided services for a competing Fortune 500 home improvement retailer's pool as well. What were the chances? I worked from the YOU ALREADY HAVE THE NO approach and realized I had nothing to lose by asking Aaron for an introduction. Long story short, Aaron helped me connect two home improvement

Fortune 500 retail professionals who explored potential career opportunities thereafter.

Don't judge a book by its cover.

One Leg at a Time

Old stories can intimidate and block you from reaching out to new people. Take small steps forward by reminding yourself that everyone puts their pants on one leg at a time. Be yourself, work on self-confidence and quit underestimating yourself. Awesome experiences - and people – are waiting just beyond your comfort zone.

I am a fan of LinkedIn's "who viewed your profile" feature. One day, an MLB General Manager reviewed my profile. I reached out to him and treated him the same way I treat others who visit my LinkedIn site. I thanked him for taking the time and inquired if I could answer any questions. He mentioned Naked Networking caught his attention. Several messages back and forth and months later, this MLB contact arranged for my son and I to have a memorable experience visiting a beautiful ballpark. We received field passes to observe batting practice before the game plus our seats had an awesome view right beside home plate. My son and I had a great time creating new memories and his inspiration and love of the game magnified. If I'd felt too intimidated to take the risk, visiting the MLB team would have stayed a dream.

Stop missing out on the wonderful opportunities and networking experiences that await you too.

Forgotten Names

Ever been to an event where you forgot someone's name? That awkward realization hits right when they are walking toward you to say hi. Don't panic. It happens to the best of us.

119

The key is to go with the flow and use some of these suggestions during uncomfortable scenarios.

- If you are engaged in conversation with multiple people, introduce someone from the group to the new contact first and wait for the new contact to share their name with the group in return.
- Ask contacts for names as soon as you realize you've forgotten. Don't wait until you get too deep into conversation to inquire.
- If someone forgets your name, let them off the hook. Extend your hand and say your name first. Make light that you forget names too sometimes.
- Own it. "Apologies, I have spaced your name. Will you please tell me again?"

Know Current Events

How much time do you invest in knowing what's going on in the world? When making small talk at networking functions, be prepared to exchange information and participate in a variety of conversations by staying current. If you travel internationally, research cross-cultural environments. Equip yourself with information to avoid getting caught off guard when different social greetings arise from country to country. When in Latin or European countries, for example, kissing can be a dilemma for those not prepared for popular cheek-to-cheek air kiss greetings. When in doubt, observe others at the event and follow their lead. Be a contribution within conversations by participating, asking intelligent questions, and sharing your opinion with others on relevant and relatable topics.

@KariMirabal
Know your current events to start or
participate in networking conversations.

Be Interested versus Interesting

Sometimes people misunderstand the purpose of engagement. They falsely believe they must find creative ways to appear more interesting when meeting strangers. The key is not for you to work on being more interesting, but to be more interested in what people are saying. True engagement means paying attention to others when they speak and validating their comments or sometimes just witnessing their pain. Take mental notes and repeat back core points during discussions. Maintain eye contact. Use names throughout the exchange and ask follow-up questions. When people believe you are interested in what they have to say, they feel respected. Networking is about active listening. Listen for clues during conversation, then express interest in helping them solve challenges. Offer to point them in the right direction if you know someone who can assist. Be genuine when engaging others.

The Unexpected Power of Business Cards

Offering and asking for business cards during networking events is part of the process, but there are other unexpected ways to leverage this tool beyond contact information for your benefit.

After you excuse yourself from conversations, use their business cards to take notes about the contact. "Sharon promoted two weeks ago to management" or "Dan moved here from Chicago, looking for a doctor" are examples of

121

personal notes you can take then reference during follow up. When you reach back out to your new contact over LinkedIn, email, or phone calls, ask questions that relate back to your notes. "Sharon, how're things going with your new promotion?" and "Dan, are you adjusting to your new city yet? If you're still looking for a doctor, I have a few referrals for you." These personal touches make you stand out in a sea of people all vying for a new contact's attention.

@KariMirabal
Take notes on business cards to spark memories
about contacts met at networking events.

The Ask: Dos and Don'ts

Networking smarter means knowing the dos and don'ts of connecting with strangers. I once coached a woman who felt burned after she referred a colleague to a hiring manager within her company. This contact lost his job and my client wanted to help. She introduced the hiring manager and candidate over email. After initial pleasantries were exchanged, her contact fell into scarcity mode. He began contacting the hiring manager with multiple calls, emails, and inquiries pertaining to the status of the open position. It became so aggravating to the hiring manager that he began projecting his frustration towards my client, after all, she was responsible for the introduction. "What did I do wrong?" she asked me. Her heart was in the right place, but she didn't properly vet her colleague or establish boundaries before offering to introduce him to contacts within her network.

Avoid losing credibility as you embark on the path of referring contacts in your network to each other. Consider these dos and don'ts in the ask process.

Ask Dos

- Invest time in asking questions of referrals before you commit to sharing network contact information
- Discuss your referral suggestion with your contact before sharing contact information
- Set appropriate boundaries that make sense for your business and reputation
- Reciprocate—Inquire how you can be of service to others
- Give credit where credit is due (reference contact and your appreciation)
- Be thankful, even if the advice or referral didn't pan out Keep your referral contact informed of how things went
- Give people the benefit of the doubt

Ask Don'ts

- Don't risk damaging existing relationships by asking too many favors too many times
- Don't pester people
- When researching information about a target company, ask for help from people lower than your target contact to gather information first

It's amazing when opportunities unfold naturally, but chances are, there'll be times when you must ask others for help. When that happens, ask in ways that won't jeopardize existing relationships or your reputation. Patience is a virtue, so err on the side of caution by following the dos and don'ts of the ask.

Make Fear Your Bitch

THE YOU ALREADY HAVE THE NO mindset can yield amazing results, but some of you may choose not to try because you fear rejection. As mentioned in the earlier chapter, Afraid, there's as much of a chance for someone to say yes as there is they'll say no. If you hear no, remind yourself that *one* door closed—not all doors. Adopt the mindset to make fear your bitch, and don't back down from a challenge. The phrase "there's more than one way to skin a cat" applies here. I'm a power networker, yet I too have received my fair share of no responses. I don't let that stop me. The word no actually motivates me to explore different ways to reach goals. Perhaps the contact needs more information or there's a backdoor to knock on. Get creative when exploring possibilities and don't give up. Stay married to the cause, not the vehicle. In other words, don't give up on your goal, just switch the paths that takes you there as needed. I've found the twists and turns encountered in the networking process exhilarating. They often produce unforeseen and unexpected favorable results.

Practice, Practice, then Practice More

The more networking you do, the more comfortable you will become. Feeling awkward is normal. Don't be hard on yourself if at first, engagement with strangers doesn't come as easily as you'd like it to. Skills do not become second nature without trial and error. The scar on my knee from learning how to ride my bike often reminds me of this lesson. At first, I felt scared to ride, but after falling several times and getting back up, I kept practicing and eventually got the hang of it. Attend as many networking events as you can to practice. Each skill-building adventure might initially feel uncomfortable, but view each event as an opportunity to test different strategies. Take what works. Let go of things that don't. Explore what feels most natural when engaging strangers. Accept there's no such thing as perfect networking. With each experience you are progressing, and that is the most important thing.

What do you have to lose?

YOU
ALREADY
HAVE
THE
NO

Chapter 6 Key Take-aways

- YOU ALREADY HAVE THE NO—adopt the mindset and take the 50/50 risk.
- Focus on being interested in others versus being interesting.
- Avoid slimy approaches when engaging new contacts.
- Shifting from bad to good networking takes practice.
- Maintain eye contact—apply stop talking strategy when eye contact is lost.
- Be a good listener.
- Ask open-ended questions.
- Engage others with authenticity.
- Don't assume.
- Keep it professional.
- Own awkward moments upfront.

Chapter 7
Dedicate

"It is only in adventure that some people
succeed in knowing themselves."
- Andre Gide

The N.A.K.E.D. acronym represents five common networking barriers;**N**eglect, **A**fraid, **K**nowledge, **E**ngage and **D**edicate. In this chapter, we'll explore the barrier, **Dedicate.** You'll learn the importance of creating and maintaining business habits, plus ways to integrate simple networking habits (in 15 minutes or less) daily to your business routine to build and sustain powerful connections.

On a weekly basis, the most common question I get is "where do I find networking opportunities?" The simple answer is everywhere. The probability of meeting a stranger who has the potential to transform into a contact who helps your business grow, offers advice, or introduces you to someone who impacts your life exists all around you. To make the most of planned and chance meetings, you simply must dedicate yourself to the art of networking. That means, adopting the YOU ALREADY HAVE THE NO mindset of going for the ask when you identify opportunities. Dedicate yourself to staying curious about where each adventure might take you and you'll be on your way.

Create Routines

Create small habits and dedicate yourself to implementing them daily. A few habits I've incorporated include 30 minutes of meditation followed by walking my dog each morning. These self-care routines have become habit and help me navigate my crazy, beautiful life. I find me-time productive because new ideas often emerge during meditation when my mind has a chance to purge negative emotions without judgement. I use the time walking my dog to pray and set goals I want to accomplish each day, including people I want to connect or reconnect with in my networking activities.

What small habits will you create to dedicate yourself to your purpose?

The "10-Second" Rule

To dedicate means to wholly and earnestly devote yourself to a goal. While for some, identifying an objective is easy, it's often the actual implementation that's not so straightforward. I find most people say they are dedicated to networking but, in reality, they've only signed up to "try" until things get hard, then they quit. To maximize your networking potential, create healthy business habits and invest time integrating basic repeatable steps into your daily routine. Before you know it, these habits will become second nature.

Early in my journey, I slipped into a routine of hesitating when I noticed opportunities. It was a coping strategy I subconsciously developed to avoid having to face my fear of talking to strangers. While identifying potential possibilities started to get easier for me, stalling before taking action made a good excuse not to fully dedicate. "I was going to approach that woman when I heard her talking about a career change, but she left before I could introduce myself." These false justifications hurt me because I knew, time kills deals. I reminded myself of the YOU ALREADY HAVE THE NO mindset and created the "10-second" rule to keep me accountable. In other words, when a new possibility is identified, I give myself ten seconds to act or risk losing it.

The opportunity cart doesn't come around all the time. When it does, I know I must be ready. I continue to practice working from an uncomfortable place of uncertainty and accept that others might reject me. I love this experience because nothing ventured, nothing gained. I stay curious about how far I can take the YOU ALREADY HAVE THE NO mindset to uncover amazing results.

@KariMirabal
Adopt the 10 second-rule to take action.

Stay curious about where new connections might go.

Recognize Potential—ASAP

Recognizing and acting on potential takes practice, like the time I noticed a man wearing a t-shirt with binary code printed on the front (binary code refers to programs encoded using only the digits 0 and 1). In layman's terms, this was a telltale sign he was in the technology industry. I gave myself ten seconds to breathe, then walked over to his table and introduced myself. I complimented his shirt and we introduced ourselves. His name was Jason. I shared that I was an IT recruiter, and I discovered he was an IT manager who hired software developers. However, he told me that he already partnered with a recruiting company in town that only charged a 15% fee (standard industry for the time was 20%). Jason told me he wasn't interested in working with any additional vendors. While most people would have just said thanks and walked away, my YOU ALREADY HAVE THE NO mindset kicked in. I told him, "My team and I fix 15% recruiter fee problems." He laughed and, in that moment, a connection was made. We exchanged business cards and parted ways with a commitment to stay connected. We did. It's been ten years and Jason and I still stay in touch and continue to support each other professionally.

@KariMirabal
Look for telltale signs of
commonality to spark conversation.

Opportunity Unmasked

Networking opportunities are everywhere, but sometimes the signs are not as obvious as Jason's binary code t-shirt. Networking potential may be disguised. To uncover more prospects, use the tools outlined in previous chapters to help you dedicate yourself to the art of networking. To recap, use a conversational tone, offer to be a contribution to others, translate intention quickly using a powerful tagline and TMAY (tell me about yourself statement), and jump when opportunities present themselves. Allow yourself to meet and exchange information with others in conventional and unconventional ways. I've met plenty of business associates at formal networking events, but I've also met amazing contacts at parks walking my dog, charity events, baseball games, flights, martial arts competitions, gas stations, church, and my gym (while in yoga pants with a ponytail at the top of my head).

People who network smarter know how to spot an opportunity that will benefit them and or their business. As you become more experienced, you'll begin to evolve and adopt the spirit of keeping an ear open for the benefit of others in your network as well. On a day I had set up office at a coffee shop, I overheard two people talking about finding investors to buy their pipeline and welding manufacturing business. Yes, I was eavesdropping. I approached the table to introduce myself because I had a career coaching client at the time who was looking to purchase a business. I offered to make introductions. At first the men were taken aback, but their second reaction was to offer a business card and accept my offer. As I walked away, I heard one of them say, "what do we have to lose?" Opportunities are everywhere, it's up to you to unmask them. Keep your eyes open and explore signs the universe puts in front of you.

@KariMirabal
Keep an eye open for opportunities for you
as well as opportunities to help those in your
network too.

Work the Room—Differently

When it comes to attending a party, my friends and I typically don't want to be the first or last ones there. However, when networking, it's often the opposite. Arrive early or stay late at your next networking event to "work the room", but do it in an unconventional way to gain valuable benefits.

Here are some ideas to set specific goals and create new business habits when attending networking events. Dedicate yourself to meeting and exchanging information with others in unconventional ways.

Dedicate

7 Ways to Work the Room—Differently

1. Arrive early at your next event to have your pick of a seat or table. Observe who comes and goes from the best view in the house.
2. Talk to conference planners or those working the event before the masses arrive. These professionals have a grasp on who will be attending the conference (i.e., companies, titles, types of attendees, etc.). Ask them for referrals and/or introductions once you've identified your target contact.
3. Most events welcome volunteers. Inquire about working the registration desk prior to your upcoming networking or corporate event. It's a fantastic way to contribute—welcome participants to the activity and meet new people. Those who work the registration desk have an advantage because they meet and greet multiple attendees. Take note of those with whom you are especially interested in connecting. Approach participants throughout the event to ask how things are going and remind them you met at the welcome desk. This approach is a great segue to a conversation with more people at a conference or event.
4. Volunteer to stay after an event to help with cleanup. Timing is everything because after the stress has lifted from hosting an event, volunteers often share information while cleaning up. Things like who attended, how the event went, did the speakers deliver, etc. These settings can offer a wealth of knowledge. As you are helping others, listen and pick up ideas about who might be a great follow up contact.
5. If given the opportunity, compliment the speaker or share with them something you learned from their presentation. Speakers meet people at every conference or event they attend. You never know who they might know who you would benefit from knowing.

132

Don't be afraid to ask them if they can point you in the right direction toward a new contact.

6. At the close of a presentation at a conference or event, ask the speaker a question in front of the audience. Stand up, speak clearly, announce your name, and what company you are with followed by your question. This one-to-many marketing strategy announces to everyone in the room who you are. It's a chance for others to recognize you which can open the door to introductions during the rest of the conference or event.

7. Leverage LinkedIn to send connection requests to those you met but didn't get a chance to talk with as much as you would have liked. Invite them to a brief phone call to further exchange introductions. Segue the conference for the introduction and remind them they invited you to stay in touch when you met at the (name of) conference.

Don't just attend events. Commit yourself to being bold in order to seize opportunities to meet people in unconventional ways. Some of these contacts will turn into fruitful relationships while others may flounder. YOU ALREADY HAVE THE NO so you've nothing to lose by going for the ask.

I Dare You: Invest 15 Challenge

Dedicate yourself to new business habits that stick by being consistent and giving up excuses. The way we behave isn't typically a result of conscious choices, but the result of building daily habits into our routines. To build powerful networks, create networking habits by starting small. Let go of the excuse "I don't have time to network" because, truth be told, we all waste time daily. Transform wasted time into productive opportunities to build and sustain powerful networks.

Stay active within your network by dedicating yourself to a minimum of 15 minutes of connection activity daily. Pick one time per day and dedicate 15 minutes to participating in networking activities. For that 15 minutes, that's all you do—no distractions. Get as far as you can in that time then move on to the other tasks required of your business. You'll be shocked how as little as 15 minutes a day of active engagement with others can boost your networking potential.

We make time for the things that are important to us. Networking is a life skill, one that will serve you again and again if you dedicate as little as 15 minutes each day to the cause. Here are several ideas of ways to invest your 15 minutes daily. Incorporate these ideas, plus add your own, and start networking smarter.

Invest 15 Challenge

- Post a LinkedIn update
- Reach out to reconnect with someone you met at your last networking event
- Share a magazine article with your online network via social media
- Share a book recommendation with your online network via social media
- Share a quote with your online network via social media
- Share your company's website information with others
- Share a career opportunity (your company or others) with your online network
- Record and post a quick video with your online network (share your knowledge on a business topic)
- Like, share, or comment on your network's posts on LinkedIn
- Check in with 3 contacts you've lost touch with

- Create a blog and share on your website or your online network
- Give a coworker kudos on social media for a recent accomplishment
- Public praise leads to private favor—compliment someone via social media for a job well done or offer a token of appreciation
- Buy a random stranger a cup of coffee to spark a pay-it-forward movement
- Send 3 people you've lost touch with an email to ask what's new in their universe and inquire if there's anything you can do to help
- Wear your "Ask me about Naked Networking" button to pique curiosity and invite engagement with others (karimirabal.com)
- Send someone in your network birthday or anniversary greetings (LinkedIn notifies you of these activities)
- Ask two people in your network for a referral to a SME (subject matter expert) to help you grow your network in your target market
- Pay attention to networking or conference event brochures; send LinkedIn connection invites to speakers before/after events and others involved in the event mentioned in marketing assets to grow your target contact network
- Post a question relative to your field or industry, inviting others to comment
- Thank someone in your network for going above and beyond for you recently
- Look through LinkedIn's Home screen for network contacts who posted a need (i.e., "My brother lost his job as an office manager, can you help" or "I'm taking my CCIE exam this week, wish me luck")—offer to help where you can or offer prayer, etc.

Game-ify It

To make the above suggestions more fun, game-ify the challenge. Print this list and throw the ideas (plus yours) into a fishbowl. When it's time to invest your 15 minutes, grab one idea from the fishbowl and do it—no excuses. Get going!

Create a 30-Day Editorial Content Calendar

Create a 30-day editorial content calendar for social media networking to keep your online activity alive. This plan of action ensures name and face reminders to the people you've selected to be in your digital network. It also creates an opportunity for you to showcase you're a subject matter expert in your field.

This "go slow to go fast" approach streamlines activity on social media and keeps your networking activity organized.

Use these suggestions to create then implement your 30-day editorial content calendar.

Build Your 30-Day Editorial Content Calendar

1. Select a unique theme monthly that aligns with your profession or passion (i.e., teamwork, leadership, overcoming adversity, managing difficult employee types, etc.).
2. Set up a spreadsheet to house your data and results.
3. Find supporting articles, books, quotes, TED Talks, and/or create unique content that supports your

monthly theme. Resources are everywhere including *Inc. Magazine*, *Harvard Business Review*, TED Talks, Amazon for book ideas, *Time Magazine*, etc. Some refer to this as curated content.

4. Create a "hook" that inspires those in your network to click on your content to learn more. A hook is a short invitation to motivate readers to want to learn more (i.e., "Curious to learn three ways to utilize your time wisely at work, read this ..."). Answer questions and respond to comments posted online from your posts. Social media is about engagement not broadcasting so stay engaged.

5. Select images to match your theme or use the ones that default from a curated content article (they automatically populate on LinkedIn when you cut/paste from a browser). Google is a great resource for finding images, be sure to select copyright free images.

6. Store this data in a spreadsheet to access content easier throughout the month.

7. Track progress within the spreadsheet. Which posts received the most comments? The most views? Mark each post as it was used to avoid duplicating efforts. Use the information as research when you create the next month's content to customize topics that appeal most to your target audience.

8. If you have a website, track views to your website via Google Analytics to review how your efforts are increasing activity on your site.

9. Recycle popular content as needed in future months to save time.

10. Add working on your 30-day content calendar to your fishbowl of ideas in the Invest 15 Challenge.

Rome Wasn't Built in a Day

Don't feel discouraged if you don't see progress fast enough. Remember that Rome wasn't built in a day. Dedicated small steps, consistently completed, can pave the road ahead for your success.

What do you have to lose?

YOU
ALREADY
HAVE
THE
NO

Chapter 7 Key Takeaways

- YOU ALREADY HAVE THE NO—adopt the mindset and take the 50/50 risk.
- Dedicate yourself to a daily routine of building and maintaining your network.
- Use the 10-second rule to avoid hesitating when opportunity presents itself.
- Keep an eye open for new connections for yourself and those in your network.
- Arrive early and stay late when attending networking events for more connection potential.
- Create a fishbowl of diverse networking activities using suggestions from this chapter.
- Invest a minimum of 15 minutes per day to stay active within your network.
- Make a 30-day editorial content calendar with a monthly theme for posting on social media—a great way to stay active with your online community.
- Remember that dedicated small steps, consistently completed, pave the road ahead for your success.

Chapter 8
Closing Thoughts and Challenge

"If you want to succeed you will find a way;
those who don't will find an excuse."
- Jim Rohn

In a world where business, technology, and people constantly evolve, your ability to identify opportunity is more important than ever. When it comes to networking, the ideas in this book can help you understand the difference between doing it well and doing it poorly. *You Already Have The No* shares essential steps to making you a better networker. It introduced you to the concept of going for the big ask because you have a 50/50 chance of getting a yes as you do a no.

You learned about the N.A.K.E.D. acronym which represents five common networking barriers: **N**eglect, **A**fraid, **K**nowledge, **E**ngage and **D**edicate. In each chapter, you learned about each block and creative solutions for success. You explored core concepts that included ways to develop mutually beneficial relationships, how to create value within your networking circles, and the importance of being a contribution-to others.

I've been an active member of my network for over two decades. In that time, I've learned how diverse networking strategies can be from person to person. Find out what works for you. While there isn't a "one size fits all" method for networking success, there are a few golden rules that you won't want to forget. You must actively engage with others, repeat what works again and again, and remember it's not all about you. Discovering something you can do for someone else is part of the fun and contributes to the development of meaningful reciprocal relationships.

Imagine

I feel so blessed when people share stories from around the world about how they implemented YOU ALREADY HAVE THE NO strategies to network smarter. I never grow tired of hearing how someone faced a fear, pushed through a barrier, took a new risk, or extended a hand to introduce themselves to a stranger. I won't stop teaching people how to network smarter until there are no more people to coach about the importance of connection.

You've come to the end of the book; let's explore some final lessons and closing thoughts.

Plan Your Work. Work Your Plan.

In previous chapters, we discussed the importance of developing a networking game plan. Keep your networking plan within reach as a reminder to commit to business habits daily. Those who network smarter understand the power of accountability partners. Consider inviting a trusted contact to help you stay on track. Together you can brainstorm ideas and practice "tell me about yourself" statements, taglines, and/or other tools for feedback. Support is important to reaching your goals. Connecting with strangers is a process of trial and error, so give yourself a break if your plan doesn't work exactly as you originally hoped. Recalibrate, shake it off, and try again.

Avoid Asset Depreciation

An asset is defined as a useful and desirable thing. You must work to maintain both online digital assets (social media networking tools) as well as traditional networking relationships. Those who network smarter understand that the process of building and maintaining connections never ends. Build it before you need it. To maintain your asset, commit to consistent network interaction—especially the process of adding value to those with whom you've committed to develop mutually beneficial relationships.

Ask Questions

Asking questions that don't require yes or no answers requires some to work outside comfort zones. Like anything, asking questions as a segue to enter conversations with strangers becomes easier the more you practice. Those who network smarter know that questions are a powerful tool for introduction. It's a way to express interest and learn new things about those with whom you want to explore further connection. Questions can lead to amazing new possibilities.

If You Take Only One Idea

If you take only one idea from this book, let it be the mindset of giving yourself permission to embrace the YOU ALREADY HAVE THE NO mindset. Take new risks, be vulnerable, and understand that building and maintaining networks is a process of trial and error. Give yourself permission to get curious about how strangers might transform into trusted business relationships. Become someone who networks smarter by accepting setbacks for what they are—setups for amazing things to occur next.

N.A.K.E.D. Networking Review

Neglect
Don't neglect your network. Build it before you need it. You won't regret it.

Afraid
It's normal to feel afraid. Practice pushing through your fear to network with confidence.

Knowledge
Use the 3-step networking strategy to Plan, Connect, and Grow powerful networks.

Engage
Approach others with authenticity. Offer to be a contribution and create value within your network.

Dedicate
Commit to incorporating daily business habits into your routine that support networking activity (even if 15 minutes is all you've got).

Closing Thoughts

When it comes to networking, the adventure never ends. Those who network smarter know that there are always amazing people to meet and exchange ideas with out there. Some will come and some will go as career and interests evolve. If you're uninspired by the people in your current network, it's time to meet new people. Networking is not always easy. Accept that everyone you meet won't be a fit. Invest time vetting to determine who to connect or disconnect with. There's no such thing as the perfect way to network, and those who are introverted have just as much chance for success as those who are extroverted. The more diverse your network, the more exciting. Remember to meet people where they're at. Some contacts prefer face-to-face interaction, while others are perfectly fine communicating online without ever talking. In time, you—and those you connect with—will experience the power of random and unexpected results that come from naked networking done well.

I Dare You Challenge

Mahatma Gandhi encouraged us to "be the change we want to see in the world." I dare you to start by helping the people who matter most to you—your family, friends, employees, co-workers, people you go to church with, your clients, and others. Develop critical relationship-building skills by sharing what you've learned from reading *You Already Have The No* with others. Join the movement of people networking smarter by sharing your knowledge, stories, ideas, and networking success on my LinkedIn page under recommendations or in your own social media posts using #NakedNetworking™.

A long time ago, I decided to face my networking fear. I gave up excuses, negativity, and adopted the YOU ALREADY HAVE THE NO mindset. I took calculated risks and embraced vulnerability by allowing myself to get naked. That decision changed my life. It created opportunities for me to meet amazing people, work on awesome projects, and travel to amazing places teaching people how to network smarter.

I wish you success on your journey and I hope you'll choose to **get naked** too.

Meet Kari

Kari Mirabal, International keynote and TEDx speaker, author, and consultant shares innovative networking strategies to help professionals leverage the power of authentic connection. Mirabal shares knowledge gathered from decades of experience. Her clients include Fortune 500 companies and executive leaders across the country and abroad. Mirabal's company develops corporate programs, products, and presentations that benefit those interested in garnering new clients, increasing profits, and advancing careers through networking.

Visit Kari at:

karimirabal.com

Made in the
USA
Middletown, DE